WHY ICELAND?

WHY ICELAND?

ÁSGEIR JÓNSSON
Head of Research and Chief Economist, *Kaupthing Bank*

New York   Chicago   San Francisco   Lisbon   London   Madrid   Mexico City
Milan   New Delhi   San Juan   Seoul   Singapore   Sydney   Toronto

1 2 3 4 5 6 7 8 9 0   FGR/FGR   0 1 0 9

ISBN   978-0-07-163284-3
MHID 0-07-163284-0

Printed and bound by Quebecor World.

McGraw-Hill books are available at special quantity discounts to use as premiums and sales promotions, or for use in corporate training programs. To contact a representative please visit the Contact Us pages at www.mhprofessional.com.

CONTENTS

CHAPTER 1

THE ENIGMA OF ICELAND

⤙ AN ULTIMATUM FROM THE KING ⤚

In the early morning in the third week of June 1000 AD, the general assembly of the Icelandic parliament, Althing, was called into session. Customarily, the session was held out in the open air, in a natural amphitheater in Thingvellir (Parliamentary fields) in the southwestern part of the country, created by the combination of lava flows and fissure formation in the earth, complete with a speaker podium.

There was great tension in the air as the 39 MPs, known as the Godi, stepped forth and greeted Thorgeir, the law speaker, as he prepared to address the crowd from the podium. The Godi represented free farmers from every corner of the country; indeed, a large part of their constituency stood behind them, fully armed. A small minority of the Godi, accompanying a handful of priests in the full regalia of the Holy Roman Church, occupied a corner of the amphitheater at a distance from the others. Thorgeir had been charged with the task of devising some kind of compromise to solve the worst political crisis the young democracy had encountered since its founding in 930.

Ólafur Tryggvason, the great warrior king of Norway, had issued an ultimatum to the young state to either convert to Christianity or face his wrath. The Norwegian king was indeed a formidable enemy. He had the largest fleet of long ships—"war dragons"—in the North Atlantic. The king's standard carrier Worm-the-Long was the largest warship the Viking world had ever known. Ólafur had used his military might to christen Norway; death and torture awaited those who persisted with their pagan ways. Now, his focus was on Iceland.

The king had sent missionaries to Iceland, German priests accompanied by Icelanders who had served in his army. They had tried peacefully to spread the good word around the country with almost no success. Frustrated, they had resorted to attacking pagan holy sites and temples and killing prominent pagans. The Althing had expelled them from the country and now faced the king's anger.

Obeying this king's—or any king's—command was not to the liking of the newly established nation. The country had been settled by Norse farmers and chieftains fleeing taxes and tyranny as the first unified Norwegian kingdom had been established around 870–900 AD. The Icelanders also knew the king would never risk his precious fleet on the high seas to subdue them. The country was at a safe distance from all Norwegian kings. Nevertheless, King Ólafur wielded sufficient power to enforce near-total isolation on the country, since most shipping routes to Iceland originated in Norway. Indeed, the king had already given a strong indication that pagans were not welcome in his kingdom by ordering attacks on Icelanders visiting Norway. And to further sharpen the thinking at Althing, the king held five Godi's sons as hostages.

To Christianity as such the Icelanders were ambivalent. Quite a lot of the original settlers had lived in the British Isles prior to coming to the country. Some had become Christians in their new country, although their children would revert back to paganism. Others had chosen to worship Christ along with the pagan gods: in peacetime they would pray to Jesus, but when things got tough, Thor was the God to talk to. The majority probably had accepted a rudimentary baptism as a token act to being allowed to be in communion with Christians in the British Isles. Furthermore, a very significant number of the settlers had married local Christian girls. Of the people gathered at Althing in June 1000, practically everyone had Christian grandmothers or at least great grandmothers. There was little religious fervor to the Icelandic paganism, but nevertheless the pagan gods were interwoven into the cultural fabric and identity of the nation. It suffices to mention that the MPs, the Godi, also served as priests or masters of ceremony in pagan festivals. The name God-i is derived from the Germanic word *God*.

When the commonwealth was founded in 930 it had been proclaimed that "Iceland is governed by laws not kings." The new republic prided itself on being able to solve all its affairs through jurisprudence and consensus decisions among the Godi. But now the issue of Christianity was threatening to break the commonwealth apart. Iceland might have had a small number of actual Christian converts, but a significant number of people had converted to the idea that Christianity was an absolute necessity to keep the door to the outside world open. Against them stood the conservative diehards that would not abandon the ways of their father and forefathers for "White Christ" as they would call him. They argued for the self-sufficiency of the nation. These two groups had confronted each other at Althing and each had threatened to secede from the commonwealth and establish a new regime with separate laws. Neither side seemed to be willing to give in. As the Althing convened that fateful day in June 1000, everyone knew that if a political solution was not reached, the arms would talk instead of the Godi.

Thorgeir himself was a pagan, but nevertheless all parties trusted him to deliver a verdict on the matter. The Sagas tell that he spent two days and two nights in his tent at the Althing, devising a solution to the crisis while the whole nation waited outside. But it is more likely that his tent served as crisis headquarters, and that Thorgeir used this time to consult with all the Godi and other major players in this political standoff.

There was a complete silence when Thorgeir emerged from under his hide and began to speak and his voice was amplified from the cliffs behind him so the thousands circled around would hear him clearly. He began by highlighting the difference between kingly rule and democracy. Kings could always act on their own whim and force their will against any opposition, but rule of the people would always have to rely on laws and consensus; besides the fact was that in every debate both sides always had something to their case. The survival of the Icelandic Commonwealth depended on the ability of Althing to contain fanatics and aggressive elements in the society. Then Thorgeir paused and then delivered his verdict: "we shall all have one faith and one law." Thorgeir argued that without the law there could be no peace and life would be unbearable. On the other hand, the one faith for the country had to be Christianity.

The people gasped. Then Thorgeir added a crucial addendum to his verdict: those who wanted to worship the old pagan gods could do so freely, but in private. After some discussion, all Godi agreed. On the way home from Althing, the Godi stopped by the nearest hot spring, and ordered everyone in their group to be baptized with comfort in the warm water. Iceland had converted to Christianity. Thorgeir had delivered a "Gettysburg address" for Iceland; the nation must never let any issue break its unity. The conversion was of course in name only and it would take decades or more for the new faith to win the country over. But the conversion would be peaceful, gradual and the church would be woven into the fabric of the nation in an almost seamless way. There is still no separation of church and state in Iceland.

King Ólafur Tryggvason never knew about this decision, since he died in battle that very summer after being ambushed by the combined fleets of the kings of Denmark and Sweden. Surrounded in his Worm-the-Long, he jumped into the sea and disappeared.

⇥ THE ICELANDIC DREAM ⇤

Iceland was the last country in Europe to be touched by men. It was discovered by chance in the mid-eighth century—the apex of the Viking age—when ships were blown off course by bad weather. There was little there to exploit and no one to conquer; the only mammal living on the island was the arctic fox.

A Norwegian, Floki Vilgerdarson, made the first deliberate attempt at settlement. The Icelandic Sagas tell us that three ravens, which could smell new land, were his guides across the ocean. Some, noting similarities to biblical stories and Old Norse mythology, believe there is more fiction than truth to this story, but whatever happened Floki acquired the nickname Raven-Floki and he did find the country he sought. His settlement was ruined by the harsh arctic winter; frustrated and angry, he returned to Norway and named the island *Ice*land in a small but lasting act of revenge.

Floki and his ilk were Norse chieftains, otherwise known as Vikings. In ships of their own invention, seacraft that could brave the waves of the North Atlantic, they became the first Europeans to traverse long distances on the open seas as they explored and searched for new land and opportunities. To English speakers familiar with their mythic and cartoonish derivatives the word *Viking* likely evokes images of bellicose heroes wearing helmets with horns. In the Nordic language, Viking simply means "pirate," and is applied only to a limited subsection of the Norse seafarers. What is more, the actual Vikings never wore helmets with horns. That regalia first appeared as a stage costume in Wagnerian operas in the nineteenth century, and from there was threaded into popular culture.

The sturdier, faster ships helped transform Scandinavian country boys into citizens of the world. Norse sailors opened new trade routes across the Atlantic and up the Baltic rivers into Russia and the Black Sea. Those who first dared explore and open these routes were risk-seeking, aggressive youths out for plunder—the actual Vikings—who in all likelihood undertook their adventure against the advice of the elders but behind them came traders and then eventually settlers. In many countries the Norse were founders of cities and trading posts; they formed the core of many merchant classes and new urban populations dotting the coastlines of the North Atlantic.

In Floki's time, Norway was embroiled in a civil war. The country was divided into many small kingdoms and autonomous regions. Around 860 or 870 one of the petty kings in southern Norway assumed the task of uniting the country into a single kingdom by his sword. Legend has that he swore never to cut his hair until his task was accomplished. He would come to be known as Harald the Fair-Haired (850–933). Harald took out the kings and chieftains in successive battles, one by one; or, if the kings managed to organize against him, he subdued them one coalition at a time. The military victories were followed by purges or forced land confiscations that aimed to unseat the old ruling class and secure Harald's regal position. He also introduced central taxation that got mixed reviews.

Harald's conquest and pacification unleashed a wave of emigration among Norse chieftains, who harbored a deep-rooted disdain for royal, centralized authority. They spread out over the Atlantic, and while always outnumbered, they visited no small degree of violence and plunder on coastal regions, often winning land for settlement, money, or contracts to guard against other adventurers. In this way they would settle down in parts of England, Ireland, British Isles and France (the word *Normandy* literally means "Land of the Norsemen") and, of course, Iceland.

Genealogical evidence shows that Iceland was settled by Norse males and women from all corners of the North Atlantic; specifically, about 90 percent of the country's male ancestry is Norwegian, while 60 to 70 percent of the female ancestry is Celtic in origin. Some women arrived as slaves, but it is likely that many were married to Vikings who "went native," and absorbed culture from the British Isles, along with Christianity. Slavery was soon phased out as the country's diverse population blended together.

The dominant culture in the new country would became distinc- tively Nordic though the Celtic element in the population would be manifested an in odd tendency toward literacy and storytelling. Ice- landers became bards of the Viking world and witnesses to history. Nordic kings, many of whom were illiterate, all kept an Icelandic poet in court as both an entertainer and historian. Of all the great battles of Scandinavian kings there would always be one or two Ice- landers that took part in the fighting and were able to get away to tell the tale and have their account written down in their home coun- try. Icelanders also exported books to other Nordic countries, and practically all written histories about the Viking period can be traced to them as the non-religious literary production of the other Scan- dinavian nations in medieval times was virtually zero. These book- ish traditions would come to have a defining influence on the Icelandic national character.

There is a curious parallel between the origins of Iceland and those of the United States. Both countries were founded by independent groups of immigrants, some fleeing tyranny, others simply searching for a better life, no small number brought as slaves. Fifty years into their habitation, the Icelanders founded what today is referred to typ- ically as a commonwealth. Their society had no head of state and no formal executive branch, but it was ruled by a representative legisla- tive authority, the Althing, which was the first European parliamen- tary body. The names, words, and deeds of the Althing's founders have survived in the Icelandic sagas, which, like the United States' Declaration of Independence and Constitution, have defined Iceland's national character and the political framework to the present day.

The Icelandic republic was simple and effective. The country was divided into 39 constituencies (Godord), each of which elected a sin- gle representative (Godi) to the national assembly. This political sys- tem, much like Jeffersonian democracy in the United States, was built from a yeoman class of free, independent farmers who could switch their allegiance to a different Godi whenever they chose (women could act as Godis as well as men, provided they had a man

who spoke for them in the Althing). The motto of the commonwealth was "With laws we shall build our country," words that are
inscribed on the badges of Icelandic policeman in the present day.

This egalitarian structure faced threats through the years, most
notably in the thirteenth century, by which time a handful of families had accumulated wealth and begun to dominate their brethren
through warfare and cross alliances. Order needed to be restored, but
rather than produce their own Caesar on the battlefield the Icelanders chose, in 1262, to form a union with the Norwegian kingdom. If a king was needed, so much the better if he was far away
and unlikely to interfere. Indeed, the Norwegian king never visited
or exerted military influence; Iceland ceded its sovereignty in order
to restore its parliamentary system to working order.

To Icelanders, the ancient founders of their nation are gone but
never forgotten. Most of them are known by name, and all living Icelanders can trace their bloodline to them through genealogical
records and a family tree that is rooted in the days of the original
settlement. The conditions of that time, over a thousand years past,
created one of the great contradictions of the Icelandic society, one
that has fueled an ancient, ongoing, perhaps endless debate between
isolationists and internationalists.

Iceland was the creation of cosmopolitans, Norse chieftains who
roamed through the Atlantic and even into the Mediterranean. They
came to the new country with foreign wives, usually acquired during
stopovers in the British Isles. These were confident, risk-seeking
adventurists that conducted daring raids on hostile territories.

On the other hand, they were also refugees, and deeply suspicious
of any foreign authority. In this sense, Iceland was founded as a hide-
out. It became a conservative farming society sheltered from tumul-
tuous times in Europe; no Viking warlord would ever risk his "war
dragons" in the high seas to carry out a raid on this poor island country. Looking from this perspective, Iceland stood to gain from self-
reliance and resistance to, as well as removal from, foreign power.

Through the ages, the nation has swung between the extremes of isolation and openness. Years spent in withdrawal from the world have been followed by outbursts of a yearning to aggressively pursue its riches.

These contradictions were especially stark as the Atlantic sea routes would became less traveled and the island more isolated as the Viking age drew to a close. The Icelanders became sedentary farmers, living on an island without ships; over time Europe almost forgot about it. Meanwhile, however, the Icelanders had written voluminous literature, historical and fictional, about the Viking age that would dominate their cultural life. In this way the bookish nation preserved the cosmopolitan atmosphere of the Viking age and their dreams of foreign countries, if only in the life of the mind.

The Icelandic dream is similar in character to the American dream. In the Icelandic version, a high achiever in any trade can export his or her success abroad. A story often repeated in the Saga literature tells of a farmer's son who travels abroad, distinguishes himself in a larger nation, and returns home with honor to work the land of his father. Still today, even though most Icelanders get wanderlust in their twenties and dwell for extended time in other countries in either work or study they usually return when the time comes to form a family or when their children have reached the age of 6–10. This is something that is difficult to explain since people often leave well jobs and positions abroad to return home. Somehow the Icelandic society creates a sense of security, belonging or self-worth among its people that can also be seen by the fact that Icelanders have consistently ranked highest among other nations of the world in surveys measuring happiness or quality of life.

The Icelandic dream also in turn informs the national character, which is distinguished by a relentless, sometimes crazed assurance today that a nation of 300,000 people can triumph over other nations in any sport competition, no matter how large the opponent looms. Foreigners often do not realize that Icelanders refuse to acknowledge that the small size of their nation could ever be a hindrance to their ambition. For example, Henry Kissinger in his memoirs spoke of Iceland as the most arrogant small nation he had encountered; this assessment was informed by a heckling he received from the minister of fisheries in Reykjavik, during the Cod Wars with Britain in the early seventies.

There are many advantages to this unbounded confidence and zealous drive. In some ways, the Icelandic nation has been almost hyperactive (and successful) making up for its disadvantage in numbers. The key drawback to this zeal is a lack of critical thinking and precaution. Iceland has never excelled at collective, elaborate planning, discipline, or attention to detail. It has never needed a strong central command to organize for war or national defense, and because of its diminutiveness, it has never required the construction of a sophisticated bureaucracy. In the Icelandic mind, success is the reward for personal daring, ingenuity, improvisation, and an eye for the main chance—just as it was in the Viking times. Its experience differs greatly from that of other European nations, many of whom (Scandinavian cousins in particular) view Icelanders' confidence as either childishly unrealistic or insufferably arrogant. When these characteristics are considered, the similarities between the history and attitudes of Icelanders and Americans come into view.

⇥ THE ENGLISH AGE ⇤

In the late Middle Ages, Scandinavian sea power waned and progressively fewer ships visited Iceland. Being without forests and ship building material of their own, the islanders were dependent upon the foreign merchant trade. They tried to ensure consistent visits by insisting that Norway, now a partner in royal union, send six ships a year. But Norway, in decline as a power, did not make good on the arrangement. The Norwegian kingdom weakened to such an extent that in the fourteenth century they formed a new union with Denmark; Iceland, tagging along, was now a Danish interest.

The Danes, far from being the strongest or most stable European power, tussled for decades with other countries that took an interest in Iceland. English ships first appeared off the Icelandic coast in 1412, abruptly ending the trend toward isolation. The British, who were beginning to dominate the Atlantic as the supreme naval power, were eager to exploit fishing opportunities and trade for sulfur, which they needed for gunpowder. When the Danish king forbade all trading with the English, and sent envoys to enforce the ban, the Icelanders simply ignored them, aiding and abetting the arrest or execution of Danish authorities. They were growing rich from the high prices the English were willing to pay in trade, and the Danes had no naval fleet of their own to force the issue.

English maritime entrepreneurs, also reaping benefits, pressured the English crown to make Iceland a dependency and influenced the Vatican to appoint English bishops to the island. The Danes, who were selling other holdings for pittances, were rumored to be willing to unload Iceland next. All the poking at eggs laid by their golden goose, however, at last goaded them into a fight. They closed their gateway to the Baltic Sea to English ships and formed a dangerous alliance with the powerful Hanseatic League, a coalition of German trading cities that wielded its own military arm to protect its interests. These tactics paid off; the English crown was not willing to support private trading interests in Iceland at the expense of other opportunities. The harassment and competition from the Germans soon wore down the English, who were setting their sights on Newfoundland, discovered in 1497, and the rest of the New World. The Hanseatic League expelled the English by force from Icelandic harbors; the final holdout, in the Vestman Islands southwest of Iceland, was overrun in 1560 by Scottish mercenaries hired by the Danes.

Problems continued, however, for the Danes; only the players in Iceland had changed. Hansa merchants copied the English and hobnobbed and traded with Icelanders as they pleased. The Danish crown, envious of the naval power wielded by Germans, English and Dutch, wanted to support its merchant class by exploiting the trading hub in Iceland. But as usual, the Icelanders were unwilling to knuckle under. They were armed to the teeth with weaponry sold to them by foreign merchants, and they rarely hesitated to use it against the Danish king's enforcers.

At last, the Danes summoned the will and means to launch a military strike. After a rebellion led by a Catholic bishop in North Iceland a large expedition arrived to occupy and disarm the island in 1551 and to impose Lutheranism on the country. There was a Danish standing army presence in the country for the next decades. The crown appropriated the fishing harbors, sulfur mines, and one-fourth of the island's farms. A new political class was created, their loyalty tied to their farms, which they rented from the king. This was but a first step; in 1602 the Danish crown imposed a trade monopoly on Iceland. Complicit in the arrangement were German merchants, who were granted sole access to Icelandic produce, with the Danes acting as middlemen.

The monopoly lasted for more than two centuries and condemned Iceland to poverty and ever-greater isolation. Severe penalties for contact with other foreigners were instituted. Danish merchants were now the sole beneficiaries of the rich fish supply, which they bought at state imposed prices that were far below the markets in Europe under trading licenses auctioned off by the crown.

Iceland itself remained frozen in time as a farming society with no towns or division of labor and robbed of its natural resources. Its people were left to read again and again the Sagas and tales of ancient glory. The Old Norse language stayed intact, at least in its written form, and old cultural habits remained. But the island was little better than a living cultural museum of the medieval age, its people unable to thrive. Historians estimate that between 70,000 and 80,000 people lived in Iceland during the Viking age; when the Danish trade monopoly at last began to splinter, in 1800, the population had dwindled to less than 40,000. There were other factors that contributed to this blight, but it is clear that the lack of free trade removed the country from the trend of urbanization and economic growth that visited the rest of Europe in the sixteenth and seventeenth centuries.

This bleak swath of history also scarred Iceland's national consciousness in ways still evident today. Icelanders are extremely self-reliant, inward looking, stubborn, and suspicious of foreign interests. They tend to think in much more unique terms than most outsiders appreciate, although it is often noted that their country has fewer people than many small cities in the United States. Inhabiting their own mental universe, Icelanders can resist outside influences and trends for remarkably long periods of time and then, once a new consensus at last takes root, shift into a new paradigm almost instantly.

⇥ REENTRY INTO EUROPE AT LARGE ⇤

Despite the threat of lashes, deportation, and slavery, Icelanders continued to fraternize with English sailors, whose vessels roamed off their coasts even after their expulsion from the harbors. More substantial contact was in store after the Danish king allied with Napoleon against the British at the turn of the nineteenth century. The British responded first with a blockade of Denmark and then, in 1807, a massive bombardment of Copenhagen by the Royal Navy, commanded by Admiral Nelson.

The blockade not only provided English merchants new opportunities to trade with Iceland, but gave a more colorful figure a chance to make history. In 1808, Jörgen Jörgensson, a Danish renegade, landed in Iceland as the captain of a British merchant vessel. He arrested the Danish governor, declared Iceland's independence, and named himself king. His brief rule ended in August of the same year, when the Royal Navy seized him and sent him to England in handcuffs; he was eventually deported to Australia. Jörgensson is now remembered as the Dog-Day King.

This brief interregnum aside, the Danes kept a firm grip on Iceland. Although the blockade had driven their state into default, the British monarchy again did not support the initiatives of its merchant class and Danish stasis resumed. This was not, to be fair, solely a source of misery for Icelanders, because the Danes, although a colonial power ruling over them, were in many ways a cordial, nonintrusive one. They were also the primary consumers of Icelandic literature products, and all the leading Icelandic literary scholars were employed in Copenhagen well into the twentieth century.

However, the Danes provided little in terms of enlightenment or advancement. Theirs, too, was predominantly a backward, agricultural society; their singular growth strategy was exporting food—primarily bacon—to Britain. Their government dealt with Iceland in an arbitrary, unilateral manner that caused constant friction and suspicion of even good deeds.

After nearly 500 years of domination, Icelanders had begun to doubt that they would ever be given equal partnership by the Danes in this union. For their part, the Danes considered their trusts to be arrogant, archaic, ungrateful, and impervious to negotiation. The two nations spent most of the nineteenth century arguing about self-governance, while little economic development was visited on Iceland. Finally, in 1874, the Danish king granted Iceland a constitution, which granted both legislative and budgetary powers to the Althing. Modernity was at last creeping toward the island.

In 1889, a new "English Age" dawned when U.K. ships of a new design appeared off the coast. The English were pioneers in the use of mechanized power in fishing and had launched the first steam-driven trawler in 1881. A decade later, these vessels were wetting their nets in Icelandic waters. The new English presence was hardly welcome, however, as their boats charged into established coastal fishing grounds and simply outfished the smaller ones. The island's fleet consisted mainly of small, open boats that hugged the coast, a method that allowed easy access to the catch but also revealed Iceland's economic backwardness. Icelanders were forced to modernize their fleet to remain competitive.

Commercial relations between the two countries, which had been tightening ever since the Danish trade monopoly was repealed in 1853, grew ever stronger. The first trawler purchased from England arrived in 1905; ten years later a large mechanized fleet was operating out of Reykjavik. Fresh fish was sold to Britain, salted cod to southern Europe. In typical fashion for developing nations, once one fishing company modernized, all the rest followed suit.

When the newly unified Germany emerged as a naval power in the early twentieth century, Iceland assumed an even more important position in British counterstrategy. This time the Germans were not going to push them away from the North Atlantic. Following the outbreak of World War I in 1914, all Icelandic ships were required to stop in a British port before continuing on to Denmark and the export of many goods to Danes was restricted and in some cases even forbidden, given the risk that the Danes might reexport them to Germany as they had done for centuries. Danish authorities were humiliated repeatedly, as suddenly Britain and the United States had become Iceland's most powerful trading partners. Iceland, its appetite whetted, was eager to cut out the Danish middleman at last. It demanded, and received, sovereignty toward the end of the war in 1918, and during World War II realized the ultimate end of the union. British troops occupied Iceland in 1940, and were relieved by U.S. forces in 1942; then, in 1944, while Denmark was still occupied by Nazi Germany, Iceland unilaterally resigned its allegiance to the Danish king and declared herself to be a republic.

Iceland's spoils from the war included a new friend in the West and an important strategic position as the cold war took shape. In 1951, it became a founding member of NATO, and the United States was given permission to establish a naval base on the island. Iceland also began to send its fish to American markets, and in time, it became de facto a client state of the United States and could count on financial and political support from it. The relationship was best exemplified during the 1972–73 Cod War against Britain, in which Icelanders, with U.S. backing, drove British trawlers out beyond a 200-mile perimeter off the island's shores.

The new friendship with America also influenced Icelandic culture. Suddenly, it seemed, no one in Iceland was speaking Danish anymore, even though it was the first foreign language to be taught in schools. When they met with other Scandinavians, Icelanders were now likely to demand that conversation be conducted in English. And in colleges and universities, emphasis on Scandinavian history, after the Viking Age, was replaced by academic concentrations on British and American history. With backers from the West the country saw no need to join the European Union. But by the end of the cold war, there was a shift in American interests, and eventually the U.S. government unilaterally withdrew its armed personnel and closed its base, against Iceland's wishes.

⇥ THE MAKING OF A MODERN SOCIETY ⇤

Iceland is about the same size as the state of Kentucky. Most of the island itself is made up of a high plateau with barren landscapes; habitation has always been confined to the coastal areas where the warmth of the Gulf Stream can be enjoyed. (The climate in Reykjavik can best be described as cold summers but warm winters, as the average temperature is 11°C [52°F] in July and -1°C (30°F) in January.) The modern Icelandic economy is about one-thousandth the size of the U.S. economy. Modern growth built on international trade has made Iceland a textbook case of a fully specialized economy, exporting a handful of merchandise varieties and importing most necessities. Almost all tradable goods consumed within the country are imported except for dairy, fish, and meat. A small market limits the economies of scale that can be employed, while the miniature labor force, able to hammer few irons at once, produces few exportable goods. Like all small economies, Iceland is therefore bound to specialize in international trade.

Compared with other small OECD countries, Iceland's foreign trade—exports and imports combined—comprises a relatively low proportion of the country's total GDP: roughly 80 percent. The low ratio is misleading, since half-finished goods are uncommon in Icelandic trading and the foreign sector greatly supplements the economy in terms of value added. Despite this revolving door to the out-side world, Iceland remains a self-contained economic system.

For a century, fishing was not only the growth engine of Iceland and the main source of export earnings, but also the source of essential scale economics. After the Cod War, the fishing sector also excelled in value creation, marketing, and technological innovation, and their catch increased rapidly—too rapidly. By the late 1980s, it had passed the maximum sustainable limits in waters it controlled. By 1988, it was clear that the catch had to be reduced to rebuild the stock of cod. This, as we will see in Chapter 3, had a devastating effect on the entire economy.

Ever resourceful, the Icelanders found the means to reinvent itself as the fishing sector stagnated. They transformed their service sector into an export sector and utilized the country's huge potential for power production. The easiest means for exporting services, of course, is through tourism and consumption by foreign visitors. Tourism had been growing at a phenomenal pace—nearly 7 per-cent—for several decades. But free market reforms instituted in the 1990s also allowed the country's highly educated workforce to export their specialties, most notably in health services.

Power production also shifted into overdrive. Iceland is endowed with two vast sources of renewable energy: glacial rivers running from the internal highlands and geothermal heat. Both sources generate abundant electricity, but of course the island's isolation prohibits the export of this energy to other countries. Instead, power-intensive industries have been invited to invest in Iceland and become reliable customers for national power plants. The economic push provided by fishing might well have come from power production had the timing of development been better. As it happened, it was not until the late 1960s, when the first aluminum smelter was built, that Icelandic power production increased dramatically. By the end of the century, however, Iceland accounted for about 4 percent of the entire world's aluminum production.

By the end of the twentieth century, the Icelandic population, so long resistant to change, had jumped to the forefront of European innovation and success and were enjoying the fruits of prosperity. The economy had overcome a long recession and stagnation with tax cuts, free market liberalization, and an international focus. The nation was young and hardworking, particularly in the corporate sector; the government was small and soon to be debt free; a private, fully funded pension system brought security; abundant natural resources fostered income potential and self-reliance. Iceland's creditworthiness had primed it for the rapid construction of its newest, most audacious export: its international finance sector.

CHAPTER 2

THE BIRTH OF A BANKING SYSTEM

On February 2, 1930, the Icelandic parliament, the Althing, convened an emergency night session to determine the fate of the
nation's sole private bank. The most obvious sign of trouble was the
long lines of depositors who had been trying to withdraw their
money from the bank, but the crisis was also being exacerbated by
international creditors, who had lost their confidence in the institution and were now refusing to extend any new credit. The bank's
management was imploring the government to guarantee all its
deposits and foreign obligations; otherwise, the bank would be
doomed to close the following day and would go into default.

Despite the unrelenting bad news, the Althing was reluctant to act.
Although the bank bore the name Islandsbanki—the bank of Iceland—it was wholly a foreign-owned concern. Turn-of-the-century
Danish investors had offered to found a bank—Iceland's first real
financial connection to the outside world—on the condition that they
be granted the privilege of printing the legal tender for Iceland: that
is, they sought to establish a central bank with commercial interests.
The government, which had long complained about the difficulty of

attracting foreign investments to that outermost corner of Europe where Iceland was located, accepted the arrangement. Now, barely three decades later, the onset of the Great Depression had brought Islandsbanki to its knees.

The legislators debated Islandsbanki's fate until dawn. Why, asked the bank's opponents, should Icelandic citizens pay the debts of foreign speculators who, out of greed, had leveraged the country abroad and taken on excessive risk? Was it not true that the speculators had caused hyperinflation through the excessive printing of money and turned the country upside down with excessive lending that led to a housing bust? The default of the bank would also relieve the country of the foreign debt the foreign speculators had accumulated as well as setting the country free from foreign domination. On the other side, supporters pointed out that Islandsbanki had enabled a modernized economy by financing the mechanization of the fishing fleet. They reminded the chamber that the bank held a wealth of Icelandic deposits and was therefore a lifeline for many companies that would follow it into default; should these interests renege on foreign wholesale loans, they would damage the country's credit beyond repair, perhaps for decades to come.

The debate took on the familiar form of isolationists against internationalists and in the end the former won the argument. The Althing refused to extend any guarantee to the bank, and its customers rushed on closed doors the next morning. As the news spread, the Icelandic government was soon receiving telegrams—from Hambros bank of England, Privatbanken in Denmark, and the Danish ministry of finance, the bank's primary creditors—which warned that the country would be excommunicated from the international financial community if the decision was upheld. The political bickering continued for several weeks, but ultimately the Althing gave in to the pressure, nationalized Islandsbanki, and turned its foreign debts into equity. It did manage to keep representatives of the creditors off the board of the new entity.

The equity was paid out during World War II, when the Icelandic fishing sector hit upon a new bonanza selling fish to Britain and no foreign creditors lost a dime. But nevertheless the damage was done. Although the other bank in Iceland, the state-owned Landsbanki, was able to keep a credit line open to Hambros bank, Iceland had effectively been locked out of the international credit market; its new, state-controlled banking system developed behind a shield of capital controls. The fateful night in February 1930 marked the birth of a banking order that would endure in Iceland until the end of the century. All efforts to understand the Icelandic banks today must begin at the moment when Islandsbanki was taken down.

What may seem outlandish to twenty-first-century sensibilities—namely, allowing a foreign private bank to act simultaneously in Iceland's national and commercial interests—was not considered unwise in 1900. Iceland was still a part of the Danish state, and it was not uncommon for central banks to be privately held; the Bank of England was a contemporary example. Some argued at the time that private parties would exercise more responsibility over a printing press than would kings and governments. What was more, the entire world operated on the gold standard, and the new Icelandic bank was obliged to insure all its note issues with gold. Most critical, though, was the fact that Icelanders longed for foreign investment and financing to kick-start their economy, which was considered the laggard of Scandinavia.

In the nineteenth century, Iceland had been served by a single, state-owned bank—Landsbanki—and 24 savings and loan funds. Landsbanki's management had been deeply conservative. Mortgages accounted for approximately 50 percent of the bank's loan portfolio, and the loan-to-value rate was set at a maximum of 50 percent. Danish treasuries were the second largest portion of the portfolio. The interest rate margin was a slim 1 percent, and the bank fixed rates were 3.15 percent on deposits and 4.15 percent on outgoing loans. Landsbanki also supplied funds to the savings and loan institutions, which served in the fashion of retail branches for the bank, providing small consumer credit loans. At its founding in 1886, Landsbanki was granted the right to issue a fixed amount of monetary notes. Although it was allowed to keep outstanding note issues in circulation after Islandsbanki was established, Landsbanki's operations remained primarily commercial.

When Islandsbanki opened its office in 1904, the effect was nothing short of revolutionary. The bank's equity, wholesale financing from the Danish financial community, and freshly printed notes did indeed give a jolt to the slumbering Icelandic economy. Its credit policy was strongly pro-business, with much higher interest rates and lower collateral requirements than Landsbanki's. Having spent years starved for foreign capital, Iceland was suddenly awash with fresh funds, and bank credit tripled in just three years. Investments in the fishing sector soon increased Icelandic export revenues by 110 percent. The country would come to enjoy a 15-year economic boom.

However, Islandsbanki´s arrival had benefits beyond new foreign capital: it also marked the birth of deposit banking and money multiplication via the banks. In 1900, about 70 percent of Icelandic savings were kept at home, where it sat idle while the underdeveloped economy was begging for funds. Thus, Islandsbanki's aggressive entrance set in motion the use of banking accounts as both store of value and medium of exchange, which is the basis of modern financial intermediation. This meant that, while initially Islandsbanki's credit expansion was financed by foreign loans and bond issues abroad, it could be maintained by domestic deposits as people brought their money to the bank. By 1910 the Icelandic savers had by and large brought their funds to the banks and only about 20 to 30 percent of the country's savings was kept at home in money notes and gold coins. The checkbook became the instrument of choice for making payments. To the present day, Islandsbanki's emergence remains an outstanding example of how advances in financial services can enable the industrialization of an entire country.

The core clientele of Islandsbanki were businesses involved in the fishing sector, but about 50 percent of the bank's loan portfolio was represented by collateral in trawlers, processing facilities, or inventories. Initially, most of these fishing clients were Danish, and many were quite large enterprises compared with the size of the bank. For example, the purchase price of a single trawler might be worth 3 or 4 percent of Islandsbanki's equity, and most fishing companies would operate more than one trawler. The loan portfolio of the bank, therefore, was always highly concentrated, not only on one sector but also on individual businesses. As a result, trouble for a single company easily could spell trouble for Islandsbanki itself. For example, after a decade of decent profits and generous dividends, the bank lost about 25 percent of its equity when a single fishing company went into bankruptcy in 1914. Fortunately, food prices rose steeply in Europe with the outbreak of World War I, and the bank not only recovered its losses but reaped immense profits throughout the war; by the time of the armistice in 1918, its stock price had nearly doubled.

As a rule, gold convertibility was suspended by the central banks of Europe during the war, giving them a free hand with the printing press; Islandsbanki was no exception, which meant that by 1914 it was churning out what its critics called excessive amounts of money notes. By 1919, the outstanding money note issues had increased by a factor of seven and prices in Iceland had more than quadrupled. Despite high wartime inflation, the government insisted on making the Icelandic krona (ISK) trade at par with its Danish counterpart, as these two currencies were both functioning as a legal tender alongside each other in Iceland. This shout of national pride, however, was premature. When Europe went into recession in 1920, fish prices fell sharply and Islandsbanki, still de facto the central bank, faced a balance of payments crisis as exports no longer covered the importing needs of the country. With its foreign liquid reserves hemorrhaging, the bank obtained a loan from the Danish ministry of finance to meet the capital outflow. In 1921, the Icelandic government also secured a loan from the Hambros bank of England, although at a high spread. Fortunately for the fledgling sovereign government, the recession was brief, and rising fish prices and a devaluation of the ISK set the country and its central bank on solid footing again.

Nevertheless, the sharp, short-lived recession had inflicted political damage on Islandsbanki's reputation. The Icelandic government, which had hurried to concentrate its sovereign rights while riding the war boom, was also compromised. Nationalistic leaders, who claimed that the nation could thrive without Danish oversight, had their eyes blackened when the country was forced to go begging for a loan, and again when the ISK lost parity with the Danish krona. The ability and willingness of Islandsbanki—still a Danish private bank—to act as guardian of the capital account was questioned. The bank was accused of abusing its exclusive right to print the national currency in order to create profits for its foreign shareholders, and, in the process, creating hyperinflation and national indebtedness.

The question of whether Islandsbanki as a foreign private bank was fit to serve as the central bank of a newly independent country was now relevant. The bank's note-issuing privileges extended to 1933, but by 1921 the Althing was intent on drafting a new central banking arrangement, one that either shifted the money-issuing rights to Landsbanki or founded an entirely new entity.

These financial upheavals corresponded to uncomfortable social transformations. Having slept through the nineteenth century, Iceland was now modernizing and shifting toward urbanization at extraordinary speed. The rural areas were emptying out and their residents were converging in port towns. In 1900, roughly 10 percent of the population lived in Reykjavik; by 1930 the number was 40 percent. Many Icelanders feared that their national identity was being lost, as the population morphed from an independent agrarian society to a mindless urban proletariat. In the popular mind, the owners of fishing trawlers were seen as predatory, reckless nouveau riche, who dominated the country in between its regular bankruptcies. The "Grimsby trash"—so named because their trawlers often made harbor in the British port of the same name—were excoriated for their conspicuous spending and large Reykjavik villas, which contrasted starkly with the poverty of the majority of the population. Furthermore, building the country's future on fishing, just one volatile sector at the mercy of foreign commodity markets, was seen as unhealthy by many. Lastly, there were worries that the hard-won independence was in name only since the country was still dominated by foreign commercial interests from Denmark and elsewhere.

After two decades of internationalism and almost unbroken economic progress and urbanization the Icelandic public swung to the side of the isolationists. In the 1920s the so-called Progressive party was voted into power. The party combined agrarian interests with Icelandic patriotism and cultural values and was to a large extent a youth movement. In the coming years the Danish-educated, free market-orientated and internationalist elite in Reykjavik was swept aside.

In this hostile climate, the Althing finally granted exclusive rights to print the national currency to Landsbanki in 1928. Islandsbanki was to repurchase its outstanding note issues in equal installments until its contract expired in 1933. This required the bank either to find a new funding base to replace the note issues or to gradually shrink its balance sheet. Increasing deposits was problematic, now that Landsbanki alone owned the government's guarantee and new wholesale funding was not forthcoming from Denmark. There was no longer any margin for error for the Islandsbanki's management.

The blows continued to fall on Islandsbanki and the "Grimsby trash" in 1929. At the onset of the Great Depression, two large fishing companies went bankrupt, wiping out a considerable amount of the bank's equity. In October, Islandsbanki solicited the acting central bank—Landsbanki—for liquidity assistance, via purchase of its bond issue, to finance the scheduled note withdrawal for that year. Landsbanki was, of course, also a commercial bank and in direct competition with Islandsbanki; although obligated to finance note withdrawals it refused, on the grounds that liquidity had already been extended by previous loans to Islandsbanki. Since the central bank was also vulnerable in the growing international crisis, it was hardly keen on risking its own solvency by bailing out its main competitor.

On January 20, 1930, Landsbanki pressed the situation by refusing to extend another bill it had bought earlier from Islandsbanki. The news quickly passed to the streets, and the run on Islandsbanki deposits began. On February 1, the ministry of finance granted Islandsbanki a small emergency loan. The following day, the bank's board sent a petition to the Althing, stating that without a state guarantee on deposits and more emergency funding, the bank could not open on the next morning. This was the petition that was ultimately rejected in the night session of February 2, leading to Islandsbanki's immediate closure.

After the Althing's reversal and the subsequent nationalization, Islandsbanki reopened on April 11 as Utvegsbanki (the bank of fisheries). The new bank had a 20 percent equity ratio and was owned jointly by the Icelandic state, the Danish finance ministry, Privatbanken in Denmark, and Hambros bank in Britain. The Icelandic state maintained control of the board, and all the creditors recovered their principal during World War II.

⊰ THE BIRTH OF A NEW BANKING STRUCTURE ⊱

Iceland had lost most of its access to foreign financial markets when it moved to separate from Denmark in 1918 and became a sovereign entity with a very short credit history. Once Islandsbanki was nationalized, there was only narrow, remaining access to foreign financing through the Hambros bank in London. As the Great Depression set in, Landsbanki found itself in exactly the same tight spot that Islandsbanki had occupied in 1920, supporting an overvalued currency while export revenues collapsed. This time no help was sought from Denmark and the gates to the international financial community remained closed. In 1931, Landsbanki petitioned the Althing for capital controls, which were instantly enacted, and which remained in place until 1994.

A third state entity, Bunadarbanki (the Agricultural Bank), was founded in 1930 at the behest of the Progressive party. Afterward, all three prongs of the banking system operated under the same proprietary capacity in state ownership. Representatives of each political party had seats on the banks' boards, and each bank appointed three governors with political connections, even retired members of parliament. The banks' integration into the political structure ensured consensus and continuity, yet kept their operations above political conflicts. In 1961 a new central bank was founded under the same political governing structure. Dozens of small regional savings and loan funds provided retail services outside the three commercial banks, but they had little overall bearing on the financial market.

With capital controls in place and the absence of any foreign financing, it was nearly impossible for any private party to challenge the dominance of the state banking structure. However, in the postwar period, a number of corporate interest groups became deeply unhappy with the credit practices of the state-owned banks, which reflected political priorities. With the continued development of the Icelandic economy, these interest groups had a growing political clout, which they used to break into the banking market and acquire their "fair" share of the savings pool. In 1953, a bank of industry (Idnadarbankinn) was founded, and in 1961, a bank of commerce (Verslunarbankinn). In 1971, employing the same methods, the labor unions opened the people's bank (Althydubankinn).

These new banks broke into the sector by opening new branches, which led to a "branch war." Since interest rates were fixed by the government, the upstarts could compete only by opening more and more branches that were close to the retail customer. As a result, the state-owned banks began to lose market share, and the country became overbanked. In 1990, Iceland had the greatest proportion of bank employees to the total workforce of any Scandinavian country, a circumstance comparable to that of Switzerland.

In 1985, Utvegsbanki lost over 80 percent of its equity as the result of a single bankruptcy of a shipping company and was taken into intensive care by the government. By 1988, the three private banks had mustered enough clout to acquire Utvegsbanki and merge into a single bank, which opened for business on January 2, 1989. This new entity reached back six decades and named itself Islandsbanki (later renamed Glitnir).

⇥ THE BANKING DEVELOPMENT OF ICELAND ⇤

Banking development has a universal logic, although the characteristics and developmental pace of different financial systems vary. History matters when we evaluate banking systems, since their final outcome has a path dependency. In the case of Iceland, the firebrand entrance and demise of Islandsbanki are key to understanding how its banking sector developed in a way fundamentally different from those of other Western countries.

According to a landmark article by Victoria Chick entitled "The Evolution of the Banking System," published in 1986 in *Économies et Sociétés* banking development can be divided into six stages, which are based on the UK's development:

Stage 1. Pure financial intermediation

An institution, firm, or individual lends out surplus savings to someone in need of funding. There is no money multiplier.

Stage 2. Fractional reserve banking—deposits used as money

Banks offer liquidity insurance to their customers by accepting their deposits, while allowing instantaneous access and interest rate payments. The law of large numbers then allows the bank to minimize liquidity risk to the extent that the deposits can be transformed into long-term, large and risky loans.

Stage 3. Interbank lending

Liquidity is efficiently distributed across the financial markets.

Stage 4. Lender of last resort facility

An actor armed with the power of money printing is able to offer insurance against systematic liquidity shocks.

Stage 5. Liability management

Banks seek lending opportunities and then matching funds. Liabilities are simply managed with new deposit creation, interbank lending, or wholesale funding to fit growth of bank assets.

Stage 6. Securitization

Banks turn existing loans into marketable securities and develop the provision of financial services in securities markets. They turn away from lending, and favor derivative products and offthebalancesheet profit opportunities.

Iceland was stuck at stage one until the dawn of the twentieth century. Until then, its market, entirely dependent on Denmark, was small and backward. As long as the Danish financial community saw no gain in integrating with Icelandic markets, it continued to neglect them. It was not until 1904 that the number of Danish businessmen in Iceland reached critical mass and formed a client base for Islandsbanki, which thrust the nation onto stage two.

Progress toward stages three and four might have been gradual and smooth had Iceland remained a Danish concern and gold insurance continued to back up its printed notes. But after sovereignty was granted, Iceland no longer had a clear lender of last resort; it was forced to beg at the door of Denmark's ministry of finance when recession destabilized the financial system.

Seeking aid from a former master was intolerable to the nascent state, and trusting a foreign, private bank with its printing press seemed reckless. But without easy access to foreign financial markets or the foresight to separate central bank functions from commercial banking, the Icelandic banking system virtually was without a lender of last resort in the 1920s. Thus, the 1930 assault on Islandsbanki led to a near-complete government takeover of the financial system supported by capital controls, and a 50-year pause in Iceland's financial development.

Iceland belatedly entered stage three when an official interbank market was founded in 1980. Not until Islandsbanki's 1989 resurrection would the nation again have a large, private commercial bank. Stage five was not attained until the late 1990s, when the financial markets were liberalized.

Being decades behind its neighbors, Iceland had no sophisticated banking tradition to build upon. Its state-owned banks had operated like any other government bureaucracies, with tight political controls that allowed only the most basic commercial banking activities under the protection of market barriers. They faced competition on a very narrow spectrum from small, corporatist banks. With no liquidity distribution from an interbank market, there was little room for an active capital market before 1989.

Once it was liberalized, the financial sector broke out of the political cage, and the older generation of bankers was brushed aside abruptly by a hungry new free market orientated and internationalist generation. Most of these people were born in the years between 1966 and 1976, and they had grown up with antipathy for politics and regulation. They adopted the American-style investment-brokerage banking model that came to dominate the Icelandic banking sector at the turn of the twenty-first century. At the time, few saw a dangerous parallel to the 1920s, when the sector last had lacked a clearly defined lender of last resort.

However, this sudden generational shift did not occur at the governmental level, which sustained a system in which hierarchy and political connections superseded merit and public disclosure and transparency were uncommon. The central bank clung to the antiquated system of political boards and governors, and never hired new talent from the surging financial sector. The divide between the dynamic and international private sector and the stagnant, introspective public sector became ever larger as the financial sector fast-forwarded into the twenty-first century.

Iceland never completed the sixth, securitization stage of banking development. Its banks never really handled subprime loans, collateralized debt obligations (CDOs), or other advanced market tools, with the exception of Kaupthing, which had a small asset managing company in structured credit (New Bond Street Asset Management). However, the U.S.-structured credit industry would exert a heavy influence over their funding.

Iceland's approach to banking was far more cautious than that of any other Western European nation during the twentieth century, and the excessive governmental controls kept its financial system immature. Once it was embroiled in the worldwide investment bubble that grew in the late 1990s, the lack of institutional memory allowed all participants, bankers and government officials alike, fundamentally to underestimate systemic risk.

In the modern day, the presence of one aggressive international investment bank would have been a tremendous benefit to Iceland. But once its *entire financial system* was put in this high gear, there was trouble in store (to better understand what happened, try to imagine all the major banking operations in the United States being run by broker-dealers). Had Iceland's banks been examined independently, they would not have looked so different from any other bank in Europe. But looking at them in the aggregate, crowded onto a tiny island dependent on foreign wholesale funding, they would form an outsized systematic risk for the country.

Unfortunately, the 60 years that Icelandic banks spent behind bars were sufficient to expunge all memories, and Iceland was due for a repeat of disaster—on a far grander scale.

CHAPTER 3

HOW ICELAND BECAME
A BANKING COUNTRY

⇥ **WILD DREAMS AT THE SKI RESORT** ⇤

On March 13, 1999, all 120 employees of a small Icelandic brokerage congregated at a ski resort, just outside Reykjavik, to chart a course through their rosy future. Business had been going very well indeed. The company consistently was maintaining a 40 percent return on equity and a 30 to 40 percent market share in the burgeoning Icelandic stock market. Since it had obtained an investment banking license in 1997, the company had jumped to the nation's forefront in that sector as well. "We're becoming the Goldman Sachs of Iceland," some joked that day, but the ironic reference to an American giant was also a backhanded acknowledgment of their recent achievements.

At the end of formal proceedings, with the bar set to open in just half an hour, the company's CEO stepped to the podium. He delivered, in a clear, methodical manner, vertical projections as if they were established facts. He anticipated a 25-fold increase in equity and roughly a 15-fold increase in the bank's balance sheet within five years. His goal was 25 billion ISK in equity by 2005; by contrast, at the end of 1998 the *total* equity of the Icelandic banking system was only 23 billion ISK. What was more, the bank would open offices in many countries, and would be renowned as a truly Nordic, rather than Icelandic, investment bank. As he spoke, the jaws of his employees dropped. They looked at each other in disbelief, and then looked in amazement at the speaker.

The company was Kaupthing. Its CEO was Sigurdur Einarsson, and this meeting marked the beginning of an era of unprecedented growth in Iceland's banking industry. Not only did Einarsson's grand scheme work, but his company's expansion by far *exceeded* the "wild" goals he set for 2005. Moreover, his blueprint for growth, via international investment banking, became the expansion strategy of all Icelandic banks, and this small country would eventually host a banking system with assets totaling about ten times the Icelandic GDP.

In essence, Einarsson's rationale, laid out in his address, could be condensed into the slogan "Bigger is better." Size would provide Kaupthing with access to funding and open the door to scale economics; a bigger balance sheet would extend the reach of the bank into new, profitable venues. Employees had heard this from Einarsson before. What was revolutionary about his March 13 message was the firm belief that Icelandic success would be emulated by Kaupthing in other Scandinavian countries.

When Einarsson became CEO of Kaupthing in 1997, he proclaimed that banking should be an industry in its own right, just like fishing and agriculture. He further argued that if you had the prerequisites for running a bank—human capital, investment capital, IT systems, risk management expertise and the appetite for risk—you could operate in Reykjavik just as easily as you could in London, Stockholm, Frankfurt, Copenhagen, or New York. In a nation barely recovered after six years of recession and economic stagnation, these views were iconoclastic. Ultimately, however, they would succeed in turning wells of self-doubt into pride in record time.

Another joke among Kaupthing employees was that their bank was going to be as if Danske Bank and Goldman Sachs had had a child. However, Goldman Sachs jokes aside, Einarsson actually hoped his company would dominate a field that enfranchised small and medium-sized businesses that had been overlooked by the investment giants, the bulge bracket banks. It would provide brokerage and asset management services, leverage for M&A activities, and would take equity positions with clients. The bank would avoid gimmicks that were in vogue, such as tech stocks and dot-com wonders; it also would not place any emphasis on the fancy credit derivatives that had become the talk of the industry. Rather, the goal would be to stay inside time-tested parameters, always using traditional, even old-fashioned methods for calculating value.

Nevertheless, Einarsson did believe that relations between banks and their clients were undergoing a shift. In his view, the age in which bankers, in tailored suits, walked into a client's headquarters, presented an Excel spreadsheet laying out a plan for a merger or acquisition along with a hefty bill and then left had ended. The clients were now demanding commitment and continued support in exchange for the fees. He averred that taking an equity position was the best way for a bank to assure its clients that it believed in their endeavors and was committed to their success. Naturally, he believed that such direct engagement also would reward the bank with lucrative returns.

Of course, this strategy entailed its particular risks; assuming risk, after all, was the sine qua non for profit and progress, and the economy at large depended on banks to carry that risk. Einarsson believed that credit risk, as a rule, was underestimated by banks all over the world, even while the market risk that came from holding equity positions was overestimated. This philosophy presented an aggressive investment bank with the opportunity for an arbitrage. He also argued that many of the loans normally granted by banks were actually equity positions that did not, however, yield any equity risk premium. Moreover, risks could be calculated and controlled. Kaupthing would make risk management the heart of its banking operations.

How could these bold plans be executed? Einarsson saw all the requisite potential existing at home. Iceland had a large pool of almost overeducated people, graduates from the world's best universities who, if they worked together, could keep the risk profile of the bank at an acceptable level while making a substantial profit.

It was a heady message to convey in March 1999. Sensing, perhaps, a flicker of disbelief among his stunned audience, Einarsson had paused at the end of his speech. He watched his cadre in silence for several seconds before he concluded: "If you think you can, you can."

⊰ FROM FISH TO FINANCE ⊱

Once the mechanized fishing industry was jump-started at the beginning of the twentieth century, it accounted for the lion's share of Iceland's 4 percent per annum economic growth for almost a century. Its large, internationally active companies brought much-needed scale economics to the newly independent nation, and they aided the development of other businesses specializing in various support functions. The marine sector as such also presented many opportunities for value creation other than just bringing the fish to shore. Icelandic companies would soon excel at each step of the value chain from catch to consumer, especially in marketing and technological innovation. They also boosted the profit margins of their catches by targeting high-end consumers.

However, harvesting wild fish stock neither creates stable employment nor is it a secure revenue generator. In addition to the natural fluctuation in the catch, there is great volatility in the price of fish and of operating costs, specifically of oil. The fishing sector, which paid most of the country's foreign bills, successfully demanded protection against its inherent risks, and ultimately became the focal point of economic policy. Currency alignments were used to fine-tune the income statements of the fishing firms; but while these measures created stability within the sector, they destabilized the rest of the economy. As a result, the entire nation lived on what amounted to a share-of-the-catch salary, since the general purchasing power in the economy fluctuated with Icelandic currency that reflected the value of the catch.

After victory against Britain in the Cod Wars of the 1970s and the subsequent expulsion of British trawlers from Icelandic waters, the fishing industry embarked on a spree of buying trawlers and building new processing facilities. The combination of new export revenue and foreign-financed investment spending led to a severe overheating and inflation in the range of 30 to 50 percent. With state-imposed interest rate ceilings on outgoing loans, the real interest rate on deposits went down to negative double digits. In 1979, the government responded by introducing inflation indexation, by which loans would pay a fixed real interest but the principal of the loan would follow inflation. The indexation quickly became standard in bank lending and would mitigate the effects of inflation both in terms of lower risk for the lender as well as in representing a more stable burden of payment for the borrower. Inflationary shocks would simply add to the principal of the loan and would be paid out through the maturity of the loan, but the real rates would always be fixed. Nevertheless, the indexation would later become a mixed blessing since it severely curtailed the ability of the Central Bank of Iceland to influence lending decisions by raising the short-term nominal rates.

In 1989, the world turned upside down for the Icelanders when the stock of cod collapsed as a result of severe overfishing. With its primary growth engine running idle, the economy plunged into recession. The krona was devalued, nominal wages were kept frozen, and the whole nation took a 20 percent cut in purchasing power through a devaluation of the national currency. The export base plummeted and the fiscal situation became catastrophic. The prime minister at the time, Steingrimur Hermannsson, for example introduced the possibility of "national bankruptcy" in a speech.

As the nation struggled, a growing consensus turned away from the Scandinavian welfare-state model with a large public sector and an active state. Instead the focus turned to the Thatcherite, free-market reforms of Britain. The disturbed political climate was at last becoming favorable for undoing the damage wreaked after Islandsbanki's collapse in 1930; the financial industry began to break free after 60 years of government control.

As citizens of a small, tightly knit society, Icelanders were probably better able to transfer capital without relying on formal financial intermediaries, but the primitive nature of the country's financial system created numerous inefficiencies and contradictions. For example, prior to 1980, the nation was in the top ten OECD (Organization of Economic Cooperation and Development) countries with respect to its income per capita, but its citizens could not buy a single listed financial asset, access a liquid secondary market, legally buy a foreign asset, or realize a positive rate of return on banking account funds.

Through the 1990s, the government withdrew from the financial sector by enacting large-scale privatizations and in other ways liberalizing financial markets. The corporate income tax was slashed from 55 in 1988 to 15 percent in 2008; the tax on financial income was set at a mere 10 percent, and the tax on individual income changed to a flat tax of 36 percent. Inflation was brought down from double digits to 2 to 3 percent in 1992–1993, after the central bank finally began to exercise the policy rate as an economic tool. In short order, Iceland became the most pro-free-market economy in Scandinavia. More importantly, the internationalist elements in the society were slowly but surely gaining the upper hand, and in the next decades Iceland would open to the outside world after a half century of isolation.

The reforms culminated with the entrance of Iceland into the European Economic Area in 1994. A special treaty between the EFTA and EU gave Iceland access to the European common market and the free flow of goods, services, capital, and labor. In accord with these advancements, the capital account was reopened in 1994, having been closed in the aftermath of Islandsbanki's collapse 60 years earlier.

Once connected with the international sector, Iceland found that its values structure—emphasizing family, work, property, and fiscal conservatism—would deliver a triple A credit rating once the economic reforms were in place. What outside investors found was a first-world economy with third-world demographics. Despite the high per capita income, large families are still common in Iceland and the high birthrate leads to a young and fast growing labor force. A fast-growing labor supply can lead to rapid growth if the labor can be brought into efficient use. Iceland had the lowest unemployment rate of all Europe in the postwar period—around 1 to 2 percent—and the highest labor force participation rate of women, teenagers, and people over 50. Being idle is considered a serious sin in Iceland, and unemployment benefits are truly the last resort. Early retirement is almost unknown. Most Icelanders also worked about 50 hours a week, more than was common in Europe. This was a European country with an American labor market. The economic conservatism of Icelandic society was also displayed by adherence to property rights, manifested in the pension system in which every Icelander had a personal balance accumulated through their working life. The system was fully funded, with a minimum of roughly 12 percent of each employee's salary being set aside by mandate. The same demographic trends were swelling the labor force, since the number of retirees was very small compared with the pool of workers.

The Icelandic government also had produced a boon for fiscal conservatism, with tax cuts and fiscal surpluses walking hand in hand. After 1995, income from new economic growth was used to pay down the public debt; in 2005, the ministry of finance announced that the central government was virtually free of debt to foreign countries. Anglophilia of Thatcherian bent and Viking values: to bullish investors, it seemed a dynamic combination. Iceland even touted its abundant green energy, derived from both thermal and hydro power.

Icelanders found German banks to be the most willing lenders in the beginning. The transfer of savings from Iceland to Germany was very logical according to conventional macroeconomics. The German population was aging, and its savings had not found a comfortable home in a laggard German economy that suffered from "Eurosclerosis": the combination of labor market rigidities and high taxes. Iceland was the opposite of Germany—young, flexible, and fast growing—and in need of capital.

Cultural affinity also played a role in the match. Germans had a soft spot for Iceland, and had always shown a genuine interest in its landscapes, culture, and literature. To the Germans, the archaic Icelandic language looked like a fossil of the old Germanic tongue and they were inclined to be charmed rather than annoyed by the boastful, micronation. Germans also made up the bedrock of tourism before Iceland became known to most international travelers, and Germany as well provided a large foreign readership for Icelandic novelists in the twentieth century. For their part, the Icelandic banks never did much actual business in Germany; nevertheless, having been insulated from the world wars of the twentieth century, their relations with Germans were comfortable.

Economic symbiosis and cultural exchange helped to make Germany into the primary source of funding for the early expansion of Iceland's banking system. The Germans would also be the last friends to whom the banks could turn after all other countries—including the United States—left them to sink or swim in the collapse of 2008. When the Icelandic banks fell, they defaulted on $20 billion in outstanding debt to German banks: a rigorous test of the friendship indeed.

⊰ THE ICELANDIC BANKING SCENE ⊱

There were four retail banking entities operating in Iceland in the early 1990s: Bunadarbanki and Landsbanki, both state banks; one private bank, Islandsbanki; and a network of savings and loan funds. In 1998, the government combined several state-owned investment funds into a corporate bank called FBA, an acronym for the Investment Bank for Industry (Fjárfestinga Banki Atvinnulífsins). At that time the combined banking assets of the Icelandic financial system were around 97 percent, and equity 7.3 percent of the country's GDP.

The maneuverability of the two state banks was limited severely by a lack of capital and equity. All banks in the system had suffered severe loan losses in the 1989 collapse, even though the state provided special funds to buy bad loans originating in the fishing industry. In 1993, Landsbanki needed a capital injection from the government just to remain solvent. It was not until 1998, after a partial privatization, that the state banks were able to draw in new capital with an offering and listing on the Icelandic stock exchange. The reconstituted Islandsbanki—still the only wholly private bank in the nation—also suffered heavy loan losses in the recession. Nevertheless, in the 1990s the bank had become the main player of the retail banking scene.

Once equity constraints were minimized and friendly foreign wholesale markets became available, the three banks rapidly began to expand their lending. After decades of capital controls, the nation was very willing to take on leverage at what seemed to be extremely low foreign rates of interest. With new capital and ample foreign liquidity, corporate debt—measured as the ratio of Iceland's GDP—doubled between 1998 to 2003. The loan-to-deposit ratio of the Icelandic banks stood between 20 and 30 percent, and the majority of their new lending to corporations was done in foreign currency. Net foreign debt of the banks went from 33 percent of GDP to roughly 55 percent. The banks were still reluctant to lend to households, with only about 4 percent of household debt being denominated in foreign currency in 2003, while the figure for corporations stood between 50 and 60 percent.

By 2003, the median Icelandic corporation had attained the debt-equity ratio of 150 to 200 percent; by contrast, a comparable company in Scandinavia maintained a leverage ratio of about 50 percent. An International Monetary Fund study, published in 2005 but using 2003 numbers, attributed this difference to Iceland's lower taxes, which made gearing far more profitable for a firm's owner. The study maintained that "while the banking sector is fairly well developed in Iceland, the stock market is not" and "firms trying to raise funds by issuing equity may face more difficulties than firms issuing debt."

Scandinavia also had faced a severe financial crisis in the early 1990s after financial liberalization in the 1980s. This led to a rapid deleveraging in the late 1990s. By contrast, the problems in the Icelandic financial sector that coincided with the Scandinavian crisis were traced directly to the collapse in the fishing industry. This is what made Iceland's experience unique. To Scandinavians, the crisis was rooted in speculation; Icelanders saw it as the result of out-moded, inefficient, and corrupt allocation of capital.

⇥ A LEAP INTO THE UNIVERSAL ⇤

Icelandic law had kept investment banking separate from retail banking, in the spirit of the United States's Glass-Steagall Act. But once it entered the European Economic Area, the country also adopted EU banking legislation, which essentially allowed the same institutions to accept retail deposits while being engaged in invest-ment banking activities. As the 1990s drew to a close, it was quite clear that the competition in commercial banking, especially on the corporate level, was getting bloodier, while the margins were becoming slimmer. All of the banks were monitoring investment banking activities and gearing up to transform themselves into uni-versal banks.

In their pure form, investment banks are intermediaries between actors in the financial markets. Universal banking is the marriage between commercial and investment banking, in which the former brings earnings stability and easier access to funding while the latter brings profitability, diversification, and various economies of scale. Their union opens new possibilities for profit, as the large, retail-generated balance sheet is used to take on principal risk by under-writing securities of various kinds. The bank can also use its balance sheet either to grant loans to the corporation accepting financial banking services, or to take an equity position in that company on its own account. "Using your balance sheet" was insider slang for securing deals.

However, there is a conflict of interest. One root of the current financial crisis is the universal banks' predilection for lowering lend-ing standards in their eagerness to generate investment banking fees.

Iceland also took an active part in the worldwide turn-of-the-century tech bubble. The country had a large, ambitious pool of techies, computer geeks, and marketers who spawned various ideas to be test-driven at home and abroad, with the usual Icelandic self-assuredness. Most notable in this regard was a company called deCODE genetics, whose business plan was to use Icelandic genealogical data in medical research. It was listed on the Nasdaq in July 2000, but its stock price collapsed when the tech bubble burst. This snuffed a pipe dream that saw Icelanders making money out of one of their favorite hobbies: genealogy.

This era also marked Iceland's first tentative steps abroad. In 2000, Landsbanki acquired Heritable, a small UK bank, for £20 million; Heritable had just 22 employees and specialized in funding real estate contractors in London. It was a fine operation, but subsequent efforts to add asset management services to its product line failed. That same year Islandsbanki and FBA also acquired small banks (the Danish Basis Bank and the UK's Raphael and Sons, respectively), but these, too, were unsuccessful ventures.

The dual impact of the dot-com collapse and 9/11 treated Iceland mercilessly and resulted in a quick, painful adjustment in 2001 and 2002. The value of the ISK had been fixed to a basket of currencies within a certain target band but was floated in 2001 and as a result shed a large percentage of its value and inflation shot up to about 10 percent. An intervention by the Central Bank of Iceland (CBI) in the currency market succeeded in stabilizing the ISK by 2002.

CBI was fortunate in that Iceland had yet to pique the interest of currency speculators. Nevertheless, despite the instant relief the ISK rebound granted the indebted corporate sector, the fallout from the credit boom and bust was substantial. The banks were still licking wounds inflicted by the burst bubble: two of them, in fact—Landsbanki and Bunadarbanki—were still in majority ownership by the government, and their equity positions were precarious once again. There was little evidence to suggest that *any* of the banks could soon resume expansion outside of Iceland.

⇥ THE RISE OF KAUPTHING ⇤

A single, independent investment bank—Kaupthing—kicked off international expansion in Iceland, and its influence over the rest of the country's banking system cannot be overstated. Its success led to a wholesale-funded, outward orientation and growth in banking assets that had no precedent.

Kaupthing—the name means "marketplace" in Icelandic—was founded in 1982 by eight individuals. It began by brokering asset-backed liabilities as businesses and individuals sought to circumvent the official loan rationing of the state banks while, for example, obtaining second mortgages or financing trade bills. The debts were sold to a third party, often at a large discount.

The bank operated at a loss for three years, but it stood to benefit as the embryo of a new financial market grew. In 1985, interest rates were liberalized, and Kaupthing founded Iceland's first money market fund. The Iceland stock exchange began operations in 1986, with Kaupthing as one of its founding members. That same year, a federation of savings and loan funds acquired a 49 percent stake in the bank; they took full ownership in 1995. Kaupthing, however, continued to operate as an independent brokerage, although it interacted with the funds.

Despite the years of repressive capital controls, the nation had accumulated considerable assets once liberalization began. The pension system was the most notable example, with a portfolio consisting almost entirely of domestic assets: bank deposits, treasuries, and mortgages. Fishing industry reforms simultaneously had created a wealthy new class of fishing vessel owners, who in turn formed the backbone of the private banking business. A quota system had been instituted to prevent overfishing, but an ancillary benefit was that each quota distributed to a fishing company was also a transferable private asset. The owners could use this collateralized future revenue to leverage or consolidate their business by buying more quotas or selling them as a commodity as they exited the sector.

Years of forced home bias had created a great, pent-up demand for diversification by way of acquiring foreign assets. Kaupthing was waiting when, in 1994, market reforms threw the gates to the outside world wide open. Asset management for institutions and high-net-worth individuals became an instant growth business. Kaupthing had founded the first foreign equity fund in 1993, and had become the leading asset management and brokerage house in the country. Its international emphasis soon brought it a 30 to 40 percent share in Iceland's stock market.

Kaupthing's management soon deduced that, given the volume of business and high fees charged by international brokers, they could realize considerable savings by cutting out the middlemen and founding their own brokerages abroad. It was furthermore estimated that 15,000 Icelandic expatriates were living in Europe, and that 4,000 were potential private banking clients. And so, in 1998, Kaupthing opened the first Icelandic financial office on the Continent, in Luxembourg.

This move into Europe's banking heartland was successful from the outset. Now established as a brokerage house and an asset manager, Kaupthing soon evolved into a full-blown investment bank by focusing on mergers, acquisitions, private placements, and managing IPOs.

Kaupthing went public with an IPO in October 2000. In the prospectus for that offering, the bank defined Iceland as its home market; international expansion was described as a tactic to better serve their domestic clients. The prospectus also unveiled a strategy of breaking into "small marginal markets not being adequately served by bigger international banks. Therefore it is not unlikely that a couple of branches or daughter companies will be founded abroad in a few years."

True to this intent, Kaupthing had earlier that year founded an operation in the Faroe Islands, a Danish dependency of 50,000 people and almost a small sister economy to Iceland. Small brokerages eventually were opened in New York (2000), Stockholm (2000), Copenhagen (2001), and Switzerland (2002).

The bold, expansionist vision was largely the product of new management, Einarsson in particular. Born in 1960, he was one of the few Icelandic bankers with legitimate international experience, having worked at Danske Bank in the 1980s before moving back to Iceland in 1988 to work for Islandsbanki. He came to Kaupthing in 1994 and became its CEO three years later. Einarsson shook up the Icelandic banking community by hiring people with training in fields other than finance, such as mathematics and engineering.

Few outsiders understood what these bright but unorthodox new hires were supposed to do for the company. Never a micromanager, Einarsson's version of governance was to get the best people together and tell them to create value. This, in turn, would begin the process of attracting more talent to his team. Kaupthing had limited conventional hierarchy, and jobs were not clearly defined. New hires would not even know for certain, when they arrived, what their specific tasks were; they were left to create their own role on the team. It was said that when you started at Kaupthing you would have to find a chair, table, and computer on your own and then find out what you should do.

Work and fun were to be synonyms at Kaupthing, and workmates became best friends. Being a spouse to a Kaupthing employee was also a testing role at times. Not only were the employees expected to turn in long hours of work but the bank would also encourage all kinds of extracurricular activities for employees, outside formal office hours, with or without clients. There was always something to celebrate on Friday nights! Indeed, Einarsson's colleagues would joke that he did not have any friends, just employees. He fostered a corporate culture of loyalty and pride so intense that Kaupthing employees were tagged "Hitler Youth" by the other banks, since they supported their management unconditionally and propounded the belief that theirs was the best bank walking. Self-interest was an underpinning for the loyalty, as well: bank policy called for employees to own approximately 9 percent of company stock, with the bank itself providing the financing required for the purchase. As the bank grew, people in key positions became larger holders of both equity and debt.

⇥ THE VIRTUOUS CYCLE OF EXPANDING ABROAD ⇤

Einarsson's speech at the ski resort in March 1999 touched off a fundamental restructuring at Kaupthing. The bank was transformed from a rather lean brokerage and asset management operation, with an Icelandic home base, to an institution that was building a large balance sheet through acquisitions. The objective was to become no less than "a leading Nordic investment bank."

One reason for the expansion was to enable Kaupthing to meet the threat posed by the universal banks. As almost the sole independent investment bank, Kaupthing was beginning to feel pressure as the three universals moved aggressively into investment banking activities, using the weight of their balance sheets. All three had obtained an investment grade rating, and all seemed to have almost an unlimited access to foreign wholesale funding. Kaupthing was forced to commit its balance sheet to maintain its advantages in investment banking.

But there were tangible benefits to diversifying outside of Iceland as well. Credit agencies were concerned about the small size and volatility of the Icelandic market, dependent as it remained on a few export industries; any move to build solid revenue bases by extending operations into other countries was applauded. Moreover, as a larger bank, Kaupthing would not only be more diversified; it would also have greater market share and pricing power and an increased ability to withstand downturns and asset writedowns.

International expansion was seen as a virtuous process in which one plus one would be greater than two, since the addition of any foreign entity almost automatically improved the access to and price of funding. Diversification could also help Kaupthing keep its corporate customers at home. These entities were becoming more internationally orientated as they grew, and their business could be lost to foreign investment banks.

The Icelandic stock market had developed to the point where it was now possible to finance growth through foreign acquisitions by means of new stock offerings. Kaupthing had won the trust and support of the managers of sizeable Icelandic pension funds, which in turn became the bedrock of the bank's support for its stock offerings. The bank knew that its success in Luxembourg depended on a critical mass provided by its Icelandic customers. But it also had discovered that building new operations from scratch, on the back of the existing brokerage and asset management business, was a slow, laborious process.

Timing was another key factor. The bank had opened an office in New York just months before the dot-com bubble burst in 2000, which dimmed the promise of the American market for all new investment banks. Kaupthing's brokerage operation, focused on selling Scandinavian equities to American institutional investors, continued to be viable but the bank gave up on its plans to expand into to the United States.

Scandinavia was where Kaupthing chose to double down on its growth efforts. In 2001 and 2002 it acquired two brokerages in Sweden and Finland, each commanding a 2 to 3 percent share in the stock market in its country. In the same year, the bank made a bid for a small Swedish investment bank, JP Nordiska. The bid turned into Kaupthing's first and only hostile takeover. It sparked an ugly fight with the Swedish establishment, fueled by newspaper headlines that shouted "Icelanders Go Home—This Is Not a Fish Market" and other similar greetings. (In general, Kaupthing strove for cooperation with the management of its acquisitions, viewing the purchase of human capital as financial assets.)

⇥ THE PRIVATIZATION OF THE BANKING SYSTEM ⇤

The Icelandic government finally decided in 2002 to solicit bids on its shares of Landsbanki and Bunadarbanki. FBA had been sold to Islandsbanki in 2000. This was a sudden reversal of the authorities' earlier goals for diversified ownership. More importantly, the controlling stakes in the two banks were sold to leveraged holding companies, and thereby set a precedent. From then on, a symbiotic—or incestuous—relationship between banks and their owners would define the nation's financial market.

These sales, not surprisingly, were rankly political in nature. In October, the government suddenly decided to sell its 45.8 percent of Landsbanki's shares to the third-highest bidder: Samson Holding. Samson was then owned by a trio of businessmen who recently had sold a beer factory in St. Petersburg, Russia, to Heineken for $400 million, which was eventually reduced to $300 million due to earn-out; the trio received a personal windfall estimated $180 million. Two of the men—father and son Björgólfur Gudmundsson and Björgólfur Thor Björgólfsson—later bought out their partner and became the controlling owners of the bank.

The Icelandic FSA was reluctant to approve the deal and deferred its decision for four months. For one thing, it was troubling that the bank should be owned by a leveraged holding company, with the state providing 70 percent vendor financing, and many looked askance at the prospect of these investors controlling a bank. Nevertheless, on February 3, 2003, the sale was approved.

Gudmundsson the elder (born in 1941) was a grandfatherly character with white hair, who wore striped suits, and had a colorful past. A philanthropist, he came to enjoy great popularity as Landsbanki's chairman of the board. He had been the managing director of a shipping company, Hafskip, which defaulted in 1985, taking the Utvegsbanki (bank of fisheries) down with it. He and other executives from Hafskip were detained and later charged with bookkeeping offenses; Gudmundsson got off with a 12-month suspended sentence in 1991. The "Hafskip affair" is a saga unto itself, which came to a boil in a very politically charged atmosphere. Disagreements about its nature abound in Iceland to this day: Some see Gudmundsson as a victim, persecuted by the political and business elite of the time.

After that entanglement, Gudmundsson, among other things, founded a rehabilitation clinic for alcoholics before investing in the Russian brewing business with his son. They bought an obsolete factory in the north of Iceland and had it transported to and assembled in St. Petersburg. Success came as trends shifted and Russians switched over from vodka to beer as a favorite tipple. This triumph in the East brought vindication for Gudmundsson at home.

His son, Björgólfur Thor Björgólfsson (born in 1967), was a shrewd investor, with a business degree from New York University. Besides Landsbanki, he obtained a controlling stake in Straumur Burdaras, another Icelandic investment bank that would co-invest with him on various projects in Europe. He also owned an investment company, Novator Partners, which concentrated on dicey political areas, such as Eastern Europe, and cashed in when the area developed. A muscular man always moving in brisk manner, he habitually wore an open shirt in business meetings, as if he was impatient to begin nightclubbing. But he enjoyed some accolades as well, such as being chosen one of the 100 handsomest millionaires in the world. At his fortieth-birthday party, held in Jamaica, the American rapper 50 Cent entertained the guests.

The Landsbanki acquisition helped make both father and son fabulously rich. The son became Iceland's first official billionaire in 2005; in 2007 he was ranked as the 249th-richest person in the world by *Forbes* magazine, with a net worth of $3.5 billion. His father—799th on the list—had achieved notoriety in England as the owner of West Ham, a soccer club in London.

Next, the government sold its remaining shares in Bunadarbanki. The buyer was the so-called S-group, a coalition of investors with ties to the once-mighty Icelandic cooperative movement and the once isolationist Progressive Party. In this sale, however, the highest bid was taken.

The press judged the privatizations to be political bargains. The two parties that formed a coalition government at the time—Independents and Progressives—had been allowed to pick their champion. This process will be discussed further in Chapter 6.

However, neither group of new owners could boast of any banking experience, and they both entered merger discussions with Kaupthing soon after the deals went through. Kaupthing was interested in Bunadarbanki, which, though it was headed by politically appointed CEOs, was de facto managed by the charismatic Sigur-jón Árnason (born in 1966). An engineer by training, with advanced degrees from both the University of Minnesota and Technische Universität Berlin and an exceptional scholarly record, Árnason also commanded intense respect and loyalty among his employees. Unlike Einarsson he was a micromanager, and a superb one. Tellingly, many quipped that no one in the bank bought so much as a pen without Árnason's approval; should he die in a plane crash, said others, the entire business plan of the bank would unravel.

A remarkably persuasive man, he would draw graphs and write numbers at furious speed while talking, and he kept talking until he had convinced his audience that he was right. Critics dismissed him as a number cruncher with bloated self-esteem; they felt he was better suited to the engine room of the vessel rather than the bridge. His judgment of people was also considered to be very lacking behind his judgment of numbers.

Perhaps it was no surprise, then, that Árnason became uneasy as talks between Bunadarbanki and Kaupthing progressed. He could not see much room for himself inside Kaupthing's tightly knit management. Soon he negotiated with the new owners of Landsbanki, and subsequently took its CEO position with about 50 Bunadarbanki employees in tow.

Árnason struck a note of asperity by maintaining that his people were bankers who had expanded into investment banking, while Kaupthing was managed by *brokers* who had gone into banking. Einarsson, for his part, declared that Kaupthing's bank's takeover of Bunadarbanki was a success in no small part because Árnason and his followers had jumped ship; it had among other things saved Kaupthing costly restructuring costs.

Under Árnason's stewardship, Landsbanki became an aggressive investment operation that at first focused on growing its Icelandic market share. But it soon followed in Kaupthing's footsteps into foreign expansion, emulating their strategy with about a two- to three-year lag. Landsbanki's growth plan in 2003–2006 had been similar to

Kaupthing's efforts two to three years earlier: acquire small brokerages on which investment banking operations were going to be built almost from scratch. However, the greatest difference between the two banks was that Kaupthing's operation abroad relied almost solely on local talent in each market. Landsbanki would to a greater extent use Icelanders and relocate them abroad, although manpower in the acquired subsidiaries was of course foreign. Just as Kaupthing had earlier, Landsbanki found the strategy of building from scratch to be unfulfilling and from 2006 onwards changed its course to considering larger targets. The two banks viewed each other as being the main competitors in the Icelandic market. The banks seldom cooperated on specific deals, and their managers routinely accused the other side of dirty tricks.

When the merger was completed in 2003, Kaupthing finally met the definition of a universal bank and reaped rich rewards in terms of access to funding. Kaupthing had been unrated, but the Agricultural Bank had an A3 rating from Moody's. The marriage of purely Icelandic retail banking with Kaupthing's foreign operations gave the new entity an upgrade to A2.

In 2004, Kaupthing acquired the Danish corporate bank FIH. The third-largest in that country, FIH specialized in lending small to medium-sized Danish businesses and had a reputation as a very conservative bank with a very high-quality loan book. The bank had served 5,000 corporate clients; Kaupthing intended to offer them new services and, in turn, use them as a platform for building investment banking activities in Denmark. The addition of FIH doubled the balance of Kaupthing and was financed with the largest-recorded offering ever carried out in the Icelandic stock market: an amount that represented 4 percent of Iceland's GDP. The acquisition netted an upgrade to A1 from Moody´s investors, once again strengthening the funding position of the group.

The acquisition of FIH in 2004 marked a watershed in Icelandic banking. In just three years, Kaupthing had transformed itself from a small, unrated investment bank into the largest bank in the nation, endowed with an A1 rating and an international investment banking platform. The other two remaining Icelandic banks saw the writing on the wall. Both began to emulate Kaupthing's strategy and expanded internationally. Kaupthing's status within Icelandic society, as the company that "had really made it abroad," was without parallel. It had become the standard-bearer of foreign expansion and the source of unbounded national pride. The success of the offering also points to the dangers of this strategy: most likely a substantial part of the equity offering was debt financed.

FIH was never fully integrated into Kaupthing, and remained a separate, fire-walled entity. Its management had welcomed the Icelandic takeover, since the former owner had been a Swedish bank (Swedbank) and the relationship had been tense. But FIH displayed a selective cooperation with Kaupthing, and the bank maintained its own brand name and a separate funding structure.

For all the joy at home, Iceland's expansion would later create resentment in its host country. Many Danes were reluctant to accept their former underlings, the rustic fishermen of Iceland, as the owners of a Danish corporation. Their press treated the Icelanders coolly and, among other things, first printed rumors that the Icelanders were laundering money for the Russian mafia. Although baseless, these rumors received wide circulation. In 2006, Kaupthing sued a Danish newspaper in London for spreading false rumors and won a large settlement out of court.

⇥ LONDON CALLING ⇤

The financial markets of Scandinavian countries are only marginally integrated and display a strong home bias. A Danish investor will not buy Swedish stocks and vice versa. The effective financial center for investment banking in Scandinavia is London; any bank hoping to dominate Nordic countries needed a UK base. Kaupthing had built operations up organically in that country since 2003. In 2005, it acquired the small London-based investment bank Singer & Friedlander. S&F was founded in 1907 as a merchant bank, and is probably best known for having employed George Soros as a currency trader in the 1950s. S&F concentrated on multipurpose banking for small businesses and high-net-worth individuals, but kept a hand in asset management and asset financing.

As a private equity house, Kaupthing made important headway in the early phase of its expansion, when conditions in international markets were favorable. It was a lean, mean bank with a very low cost-to-income ratio. In 2006, it was ranked as the second-most-efficient bank in Europe (out of 51) by the international management consulting firm Arthur D. Little.

After the acquisition of Bunadarbanki in 2003, Einarsson stepped down as CEO and became chairman of the board. The successor, Hreidar Már Sigurdsson (born 1970) had served as Einarsson's deputy since 1998. Sigurdsson was a quick thinker and fast talker, with an eye for numbers and a genuine dealer's instinct, who had begun at Kaupthing at the same time as Einarsson in 1994. The two were an effective team, as they were almost the complete opposites of each other. As the bank grew in size, the original, tight circle of management came to be seen as an impenetrable clique; new arrivals sometimes felt they could not become part of the decision-making process. Later on this close knit group would be criticized for having isolated themselves from the intense creative and interactive processes that had been the cornerstone of the bank in the beginning and that they had consequently abandoned critical thinking.

Freed from his executive responsibilities, Einarsson commanded respect in Iceland, but was never exactly popular. He became the poster boy for corporate greed due to the fat stock options the bank's board had granted him and his top brass. The banking expansion in general was defined as the age of "supersalaries." Stock options and bull markets created immense wealth for select employees. This, too, rankled the egalitarian spirit, but it attracted the best graduates in business, law, engineering, and economics. Young, energetic, confident, yet inexperienced, this generation provided the muscle behind the age of leveraged buyouts. The Icelandic banking community became a testosterone-filled world of self-assured people who had an affinity for bold plans and who would reap extraordinary gains in the first years of the expansion.

Under Einarsson's stewardship, Kaupthing roughly doubled in size in every year from 1995 to 2006. However, after the banking collapse, he would be criticized for his obsession with growth and expansion. Einarsson was in essence a visionary with limited attention to details. He was derided as bullheaded, with 17 gears for forward but none for reverse.

Kaupthing's attempt to export its culture through the acquisition of financial companies abroad had mixed success. Its goal was achieved, to a large extent, in Britain, but never flew in Scandinavia. Many in Kaupthing's management later commented that the expansion into Scandinavia was a mistake, given the very hostile reception it received; from the outset, thought the critics, London should have been the bank's primary focus.

As stated, this phase of Icelandic development has a close parallel to changes in the American investment banking that followed the repeal of the Glass-Steagall Act in 1999. Traditionally, U.S. deal brokers had been reluctant to hold risky assets on their balance sheet, endowed as they were with less capital and being less inclined to assume "principal" risk. After Glass-Steagall was overturned, brokers realized that they would need to commit their balance sheets to deals if they were to compete with giants such as Citigroup and JP Morgan Chase. Since they could not accept retail deposits, they enlarged their balance sheets via wholesale markets and funded illiquid assets with long-term debt and equity.

These methods produced enormous profits from 1998 to 2007, when markets were sound and funding was easy to procure. When the subprime crisis hit the financial market, wholesale funding quickly dried up, and the bulge-bracket banks found it difficult to secure funding for their oversized balance sheets. Winding down by selling their assets was also nearly impossible, as no counterparty could be found. Since then, the five largest American investment banks have declared bankruptcy, had a "shotgun wedding" with a commercial bank, or transformed themselves into a universal bank via a bank holding company.

By contrast, the Icelandic banks could accept retail deposits, but their home market was extremely small. In the end, their strategy for profit and expansion was essentially the same that U.S. investment banks employed: the use of wholesale markets funding to build a large balance as an instrument for attracting investment banking fees. Therefore, the fate of the Icelandic banks and the U.S. investment banks became intertwined both in sickness and in health.

The Icelandic brand of investment banking was described as follows by UBS Equity Investment Research in a December 5, 2007, report titled "Icelandic Banks: A Question of Risk-Reward." (This report remains the best primer on the business model of the Icelandic banks.)

"Icelandic banks differ from other European banks through their aggressive expansion outside their home market, their entrepreneurial, almost private-equity-like approach, and the fact that they have almost no legacy in any of the markets that they enter. Icelandic bank earnings are largely made up of corporate and investment banking (CIB) and private equity earnings against the backdrop of a local stock market that has outperformed substantially. The banks are well managed and have established a track record as savvy investors. Their disclosure is generally good but could be improved with regard to segmental disclosure and equity investments."

The Nordic banking market is, on the other hand, dominated by medium-sized retail-corporate banks that tend to be relatively risk averse in their lending to clients. That is the legacy from the severity of the Scandinavian banking crisis in the early 1990s. The Icelandic banks differed from this model by creating far wider, pan-European networks, which included a significant earnings proportion from investment banking and private equity. Their aggressive tactics, most akin to American broker-dealers, were bound to stir resentment in Scandinavia.

CHAPTER 4

THE GEYSER CRISIS

⊰ THE CANARY IN THE COAL MINE ⊱

Early on March 30, 2006, about 30 credit investors paid a visit to Kaupthing's headquarters in Reykjavík. The group was hosted by Barclays Capital, which had arranged a road show for individuals eager to meet the leaders of Iceland's financial community.

The meeting, which began cordially, soon became unruly. The investors tired of listening to Kaupthing's management and subjected the CEO Sigurdsson to a barrage of hostile questions and loud interruptions. "This is not a bank but a hedge fund!" exclaimed one gentleman.

After the Barclays group filed out, a second group, led by UBS, was ushered in on their heels. They, too, subjected the management to barely civil questions about the bank's appetite for growth equity positions and its ability to withstand the severe economic contraction the investor's felt was Iceland's immediate due. "And by the way," went one refrain, "where will you fund yourself in the future?"

The Icelanders argued that their economy was not going down and that the bank's risk management had things covered. "We will not need to tap the London wholesale funding market at all in 2006," claimed Sigurdsson.

It was all rather astonishing to the Kaupthing officers. Even a month before, getting 30 asset managers to travel en masse from London to Reykjavik would have been unlikely; receiving visits from two groups before lunch certainly was impossible. The sight of so many foreign financiers, impeccably dressed and crowded into a single room, shouting and waving their hands, was almost comical.

Almost, but not quite. No one missed the dark undertone of that morning. Many of the attendees worked for hedge funds, and most of those recently had taken short positions against Iceland. As a result, the Icelandic krona was in free fall. The credit default swap (CDS) spreads of the Icelandic banks had so widened as to effectively block them out of the international wholesale financial market. News wires stated almost daily that Iceland was "melting."

In addition to investors, a steady stream of analysts, prominent bankers, and journalists were visiting the three major banks. In the UK, the spike in news coverage created so much general interest that British Airways for the first time offered direct flights to Reykjavik to meet increased tourist demand. Such was the hothouse climate created by the 2006 "Geyser Crisis" (the name was taken from Iceland's famous hot spring, Geysir, which was known for its intermittent, hot violent eruptions).

The threat to the ISK had an immediate effect on the global carry trade; a sell-off already had begun in other high-yielding currencies, such as the Turkish lira and the South African rand. The following commentary, written by Jeremy Warner, appeared on March 31, 2006—a day after investors had visited Kaupthing—in *The Guardian:*

> This is the first time I've put pen to paper on the Icelandic economy, and I rather suspect it will be the last. For a country which has a population no bigger than that of Nottingham, Iceland is generating an awful lot of column inches right now. That's . . . because the economy seems to be going down the drain. In normal circumstances, such an event would go almost wholly unrecorded on these shores. The reason

it takes on a deeper significance is that much the same thing seems to be happening in an array of similarly once buoyant smaller economies—Eastern Europe, Turkey, Israel and New Zealand. The effect of high interest rates in these countries relative to the big developed economies has been to attract a wall of hot, international money, able to borrow cheap and lend a lot more expensively. This in turn has fuelled a boom in domestic demand. The success of these so-called "carry trades" depends vitally on the currency remaining strong. The moment it wavers, as has happened in all these countries with the economic boom reaching unsustainable levels, the capital takes flight. Yet at this stage there seems little reason to believe the effect will be more widespread. The losses being incurred by international capital in the likes of Iceland are too small to threaten wider systemic failure. Most bankers remain of the view that the situation is containable. Credit conditions are tightening globally, but there is no reason to believe these little local difficulties will result in a fully blown credit crunch.

The crisis had two points of origin: aggressive international expansion by the banks and overheating of the nation's economy along with a ballooning carry trade. Kaupthing was the first to demonstrate how risk diversification by way of acquisitive growth could create a self-reinforcing, virtuous cycle that delivered higher credit ratings and economies of scale. The other two banks followed suit. When Landsbanki made its first acquisitions in the UK in 2005, it watched its Moody's rating rise from A3 to A2. Islandsbanki similarly picked up a retail bank in Norway.

The domestic deposit base was too small to finance the international expansion; it was in fact hard-pressed to supply even sufficient equity. All three banks therefore returned to the seemingly endless liquidity pool of foreign wholesale markets, to which their excellent credit ratings gave them access. Combined, the three banks issued EUR 15 billion worth of new debt in 2005, an amount considerably larger than the total GDP of Iceland.

These funds were drawn almost exclusively from the European MTN (medium-term note) market. The MTN was created by General Motors in the early 1970s as an extension of the commercial paper market. It had become the vehicle of choice for large companies and even governments to pay for their medium-term financing needs. MTNs are typically noncallable, unsecured, senior debt securities, with fixed coupon rates and investment-grade credit ratings that are not listed, but rather sold directly to investors.

The Icelandic banks discovered they could also exploit the country quotas that banks and investment funds kept in their portfolios. The quotas were maintained for assets with risk that ran idiosyncratic to the international financial market, and thus incrementally decreased the total risk of their portfolio adjusted for return. Since the Icelandic sovereign was debt free and created no need to issue foreign bonds, the quota spaces were completely empty, waiting for an Icelandic bank to fill them in.

The MTN issuing in 2005 saw the three banks racing to capture these country quotas, which in turn led them to oversupply the European market. It was only a question of time before investors assessed the banks as representing the same credit risk coming from the same financial system. Once their accumulated debt was totaled and compared with the GDP of Iceland, many began wondering if Icelanders had jumped out of their league.

While the banks' acquisitions of foreign subsidiaries could stabilize the revenue stream, diversify the asset base, and look good for stockholders and rating agencies, credit investors, looking at the banks from the liability side, saw weaknesses in their expansion strategy. The foreign subsidiaries were regulated as separate entities and could not bleed liquidity to the parent company in time of need. For example, Kaupthing could not move funds from the Danish FIH to relieve financial distress. No matter how international the banks claimed to be, in the end the credit investors always had a claim on the parent bank in Iceland.

Moreover, the acquisition might lead to greater risk exposure at the parent bank. Adding new units with conservative credit policies enlarged the total of the parent bank's capital base and gave it increased scope for taking private or public equity positions in Iceland or anywhere else. Kaupthing's policy kept total equity positions below 35 percent of risk capital, but unlisted equity exposure could at maximum reach 15 percent of risk capital. But while it had doubled its balance sheet by acquiring FIH, the Danish bank's large corporate loan book also doubled Kaupthing's potential for private equity positions at the parent bank in Iceland.

Despite the potential for trouble down the road, the ICEX was booming, rising 59 percent in 2004 and 65 percent in 2005. All three banks had been riding the wave and reported about 40 percent return of equity in 2005 compared with the European average of about 15 percent return on equity. But the boom was also bound to draw skeptical attention from the international credit market.

The average credit investor in the European MTN market knew little of Iceland beyond what she or he might find in tourist brochures. When investors' curiosity was piqued, it was next to impossible for them to procure information, since there was no newswire consistently reporting in English from this remote and mysterious island nation. In 2005, a new metric suddenly gave the skeptics the means to express their bearishness by taking short positions against Icelandic banks. This was the so-called credit default swap (CDS); as it was popularized, it became the red flag that drew international attention to Iceland and set the 2006 crisis in motion.

The CDS is a credit derivative contract, in which the buyer insures a certain financial asset against default by paying a certain premium; the CDS spread is comparable to the yield on a bond. The widening of a company's CDS spread is thus an indicator of a higher probability of default, as well as higher cost of credit if the company wishes to issue more debt, or refinance. This type of derivative contract was first issued by JP Morgan in 1997, and all issuers took care to call it a credit default swap, rather than credit default insurance, since the market for insurance was subject to regulation. Therefore, the CDS trade was an over-the-counter market with no visibility as to real volumes or participants. What was more, the absence of regulation suggested that anyone with sufficient financial capacity could sell or buy default insurance, without ever possessing the financial asset itself.

To grasp the implications of this, consider that if the conventional insurance market operated in the same, unregulated manner, it would be possible for one—or many—persons to insure a house they do not own. Thus the claim on the insurance company would be a multiple of the actual worth of the house and, should it be burned down, all the insurers would be able to pocket a sizable gain. Little wonder, then, that Warren Buffett has called credit default swaps "financial weapons of mass destruction." They offer a convenient way of shorting bonds and make it possible to build up a volume of contracts that far exceed the value of the bond in question, but they also create a perverse incentive when many parties stand to gain from a company's default.

The CDS market can be especially lethal for banks, since the spread indicates not only funding costs but also market confidence. Banks must borrow money to relend to their clients, usually with a relatively thin margin, and must have a constant access to liquidity. A large widening in the CDS spread thus prices a bank out of the funding markets, drains its liquidity, and erodes its confidence to the extent that a failure can easily become a self-fulfilling prophecy. A CDS spread widening, perhaps as a result of speculation, is a modern version of a bank run in the wholesale financial markets. Shorting in the CDS market of a respective company can be compounded by a shorting of its stock to double-down the negative impact on its market confidence. On small, open economies, a third front of attack can be opened by shorting the domestic currency, since depreciation will erode confidence by creating turbulence in the financial system, with rising inflation and ballooning of currency-linked debt. A hedge fund could look over these factors and think: triple play.

With all these factors in motion, in hindsight it is easy to identify Iceland as the sitting duck of early 2006.

The impetus to short Icelandic banks did not, however, come from a hedge fund, but from the state-controlled Petroleum Fund of Norway (PFN). Although it has never joined OPEC, Norway is one of the largest exporters of North Sea oil. PFN is a large investment fund in the custody of the Norwegian central bank that is responsible for investing the proceeds from the country's oil production and sale.

In the fall of 2005, a PFN employee named Herleif Havik became perhaps the first to buy a protection on Kaupthing's debt, although PFN did not own a single bond issued by the bank. Havik later explained his trade by noting that both Barclays and Kaupthing had outstanding bonds, trading at the same premium: 20 basis points over Libor. Havik was certain that the tiny Icelandic state would not be able to offer the same protection for Kaupthing that Britain could give Barclays in the event of crisis. Therefore, selling a CDS protection on Barclays while buying one on Kaupthing was an arbitrage, and he would be able to mass up an almost costless short against Kaupthing.

There is no reliable information on the volume of Havik's short trade or on the size of the market at the time, but all evidence suggests that his persistent buy orders for protection against Kaupthing were responsible for doubling the CDS spread, to about 40 basis points above Libor in the autumn of 2005. Kaupthing, which now stood out among other banks with a similar rating, was picked up by the analysts' radar.

The first credit report on Kaupthing, and the Icelandic banking system in general, was published by the Royal Bank of Scotland on November 23, 2005. The report noted that "a small number of investors had concerns about Icelandic banks" but "the applicable rating agencies remained convinced by the robustness of the major players to the system." The report highlighted the key concerns investors had about Kaupthing and the other Icelandic banks: the private equity positions, the reliance on wholesale funding, and the apparent mismatch between the maturities of assets and liabilities of the bank. Last, it was noted that Kaupthing, with a balance sheet 2.5 times Iceland's GDP, was simply too large to be rescued by the sovereign.

Credit reports that followed made similar observations, perhaps best condensed by Simon Adamson, a fixed income analyst at Credit-Sights, in a report published in January. "A stock market bubble, incestuous cross-ownership in the financial and corporate sectors, imbalances in the economy and the banks' over-reliance on market funding point to significant, and perhaps underestimated, systemic risks," he wrote. But in fact, the storm would start elsewhere.

⇥ How to Overheat an Economy ⇤

Trouble for the Icelandic economy had been inevitable from early 2003, when it was hit with a threefold stimulus: capital-intensive power projects, quantitative easing of monetary policy, and privatization of the banking system. Each factor of itself would have been sufficient to overheat the economy; together, they quickly brought it to the boiling point. By the end of 2005, interest rates had more than doubled, to 10.75 percent. The ICEX had almost quadrupled since the summer of 2003. Housing prices in Reykjavik had doubled in the same period.

The Althing in 2003 approved plans to expand power production capacity that would in turn provide electricity to two new aluminum smelters. Both were gigantic, capital-intensive projects, built on the western and eastern coasts of the island. In the west, the power was generated through geothermal means by drilling holes deep into the volcanic hotbed of the country to let out steam that would turn power generators. In the east, a new lake 54 square kilometers in size filled with glacier water was formed by building the largest gravel dam in the world. The water was then led through underground tunnels to generate electricity for a new Alcoa smelter. Together, their costs amounted to roughly 35 percent of the country's GDP.

The power companies were owned by the state or municipalities, and their investment goods, invariably, were imported. The smelter projects were bound to increase the country's foreign debt and trade deficit until their slated 2007 completion, when, it was anticipated, exported aluminum would address the imbalances. Demand on the labor market was mitigated when the general contractor, the Italian company Impregilo, brought in workers from Portugal and China to complete the hard labor in the highlands. Impregilo, not overly concerned with Icelandic labor laws or regulation, raised a "mining town" for its Sino-Portuguese workforce, which remained isolated from the society at large. Nevertheless, the grand scale of these projects was enough to produce ample economic heat and give support to currency speculators taking long positions on the ISK.

The central bank added fuel to the fire with a quantitative monetary easing which the good people at the bank maintained to be a technical thing that had nothing to do with monetary policy. In accord with European rules, the reserve requirement for the Icelandic banking system was lowered to 2 percent, down from 4 percent. This regulatory change freed up liquidity and increased the Icelandic money multiplier from about 8 to about 15. This was followed—in accordance with basic economic laws—by rapid deposit creation in the banking system and thus a steep rise in the money supply. Since most of the costs in retail banking are fixed—concrete, computers, and staff—the marginal cost of the deposits generated by a higher money multiplier was very low. The banks discovered that their branches were filling up with new, cheap funding, which was returned to the economy as new loans. At the time, the central bank seemed not to understand the economic impact of this regulatory change, as no counteraction was taken.

The final 2003 stimulus occurred when the government sold its remaining shares in Landsbanki and Bunadarbanki. Spurred on by new owners, new capital, new deposits, and new, and higher ratings, the banks began to lend more aggressively. Landsbanki concentrated its investment banking activities in Iceland, in particular beefing up its presence in the Icelandic corporate market. The bank tripled its balance sheet from 2003 to 2005, mostly by channeling foreign wholesale funding to Icelandic corporations; as a result, it was able achieve nearly a 40 percent market share in domestic corporate lending.

Kaupthing, as mentioned, focused on foreign acquisitive growth and allowed Landsbanki to increase its market share in Icelandic corporate lending. However, after acquiring FIH in Denmark and obtaining an A1 rating in 2004, the bank energetically turned its attention back to its domestic market. In August of 2004, the bank burst into the retail scene by offering mortgages with a lower rate and higher leverage ratio than had previously been available in Iceland.

Historically, most of the mortgage lending had been done by the state-owned Housing Financing Fund, which operated under a state guarantee and securitized its lending by selling inflation-linked bonds with a very long maturity. The HF Fund in many ways was similar to the American Fannie Mae and Freddie Mac, except that it has direct customer contact. Its lending was capped by a political rule stipulating that, irrespective of income or value of the collateral, each customer could borrow only a certain fixed maximum amount from the fund. This was a part of an affordable housing policy instituted by the government. Its effect was to provide low-income customers the ability to buy a house with a high leverage and cheaper rates, while those with high incomes were financed either with low leverage or higher rates. All of the loans were then put in one pool and securitized as a single asset and sold under a government guarantee. In essence this arrangement used the credit quality of low leverage loans on the middle class to subsidize credit with a high leverage to the lower income groups.

This system had been in effect with some variations for decades and had resulted in very widespread home ownership in Iceland and, surprisingly enough, no major credit problems for the lower income groups. Nevertheless, the middle class was left very discontented with the availability of credit. The real estate market in Reykjavik also reflected these lending parameters with a premium on small, affordable apartments compared with single-family housing, measured in price per square meter, and a surprisingly narrow price range between apartments in downtown compared with the suburbs.

Historically, the banks had to be content with collecting overflow by offering second right mortgages with a relatively short maturity and high interest rate. This was changed overnight in August 2004, when Kaupthing began to offer mortgages on first right at the same rate as the HF Fund (4.15 percent real plus inflation indexation) but allowing up to 80 percent loan financing.

The bank had several motives for this move. First, Kaupthing had the lowest market share in consumer lending, but its retail branch network was as developed as those of the other two banks and the savings funds. Therefore, a higher market share and more services sold, using the same branch system, would create almost costless revenues for the bank. Moreover, transforming the largely unsecured consumer loan portfolio into housing debt would also lower the capital charges the bank faced according to the international capital adequacy ratio rules, and facilitate better funding in the future. Last, as a PR move, the bank's management was keen to share the fruits of their international expansion with the Icelandic nation by offering cheap real estate loans.

Kaupthing initiated no less than a paradigm shift in the housing market. It reaped great success and a flock of not only new customers but also the very customers every bank wants to attract: the high income households unhappy with the credit rationing of the HF Fund. The other two banks had no choice but to offer the same rates. With the last vestiges of the credit controls now abolished in the Icelandic financial market, the average housing price skyrocketed.

There is though a fundamental difference between the Icelandic housing bubble and the bubble, say, in the United States, making it much less of a problem for Icelandic banks. In Iceland, the availability of credit after the privatization of the banks was restricted mainly to the upper and middle classes, which took on the new leverage; the lower income groups already had the credit access they needed and would be content to stay with the HF Fund. The housing price increase was primarily focused on real estate whose price had previously been depressed by credit rationing, such as single-family housing, downtown apartments, and houses that had some attractive qualities like a view over the sea. For the lower income groups the housing bubble came as a windfall: they suddenly owned new equity in their houses, which they might even sell to relocate elsewhere, to the suburbs or even out of Reykjavik. In the United States, on the other hand, the availability of new credit for housing purchases was primarily targeted at "subprime" lower income groups that would leverage themselves beyond any sensible means. To generate a similar credit crisis in the Icelandic housing market one would have to observe an almost complete collapse of either the ability or willingness of the Icelandic middle class to pay. That prospect is not inconceivable, although it has not materialized yet.

The central bank (CBI), still slow to respond, began to raise interest rates cautiously in May 2004. Rates were not raised aggressively until two years into the expansion, in 2005. The CBI had embraced inflation targeting in 2001. Inflation targeting is built on the premise that a central bank should keep inflation at a given target number with the aggressive use of the policy rate if needed; it has become the predominant way of conducting monetary policy by most of the smaller central banks in the Western world.

The economic department of the CBI was filled with young, well-educated, and enthusiastic economists, who were eager to put the new theory into practice and cure the country's chronic inflationary problem. While policy interest decisions were actually made by the three governors of the CBI, the economists were close advisors. When the country failed repeatedly to reach the 2.5 percent target they had set, the economists, rather than relent, became ever more adamant in their belief that CBI would have to set very tough measures to establish new credibility in its battle against inflation.

Iceland then became ever more orthodox in its adherence to inflation-targeting policy, up to the point of being much more Catholic than the pope in viewing how the policy rate should be used to quell inflation. The economic department of CBI demanded rate hikes almost up to the moment the banks collapsed: no arguments, the country was going to bow to the books and hit the target.

Kaupthing's entrance into the mortgage market in 2004 also created an extraordinary new problem for the CBI. Unlike most other countries, housing costs in the Icelandic consumer price index (CPI) were measured as an opportunity cost of *owning* a house, rather than the actual user costs of *renting* a house. This was an important difference, since it meant that a higher housing price instantly translated into a higher opportunity cost of living in a household and a rise in inflation. Again, there were smart, well-educated people at the Statistical Institute who maintained that economic theory was the best way to measure housing costs.

Overall, housing costs had about 20 percent weight in the CPI, which meant that about 20 percent of all housing price increases were fed into inflation. In the first 12 months after Kaupthing's entrance into the mortgage market, housing prices rose by 40 percent; CBI had to keep up raising interest rates.

Hiking interest rates in a small, open economy in response to overheating is in some ways counterproductive, especially if the rates are raised significantly higher than those of neighboring countries; this will attract foreign funds and appreciate the currency. An overvalued currency in turn creates false wealth effects. Households can buy foreign goods at great bargains, and even domestic companies can acquire foreign assets at prices that seem to be extremely cheap.

At the end of 2005, the CBI's policy rate stood at about 10.5 percent, which compared favorably with the dollar and the euro, and made Iceland an instant favorite among carry traders. Investors who use the carry trade will take loans in low-yielding currencies, such as the yens or the Swiss francs; invest the money in high-yielding currencies, such as the Turkish lira, the South African rand, or the Icelandic krona; and pocket the difference.

The carry trade is a deeply leveraged, high-risk game that lures players with the chance for enormous profits. Most high-yielding currencies are traded in small, illiquid currency markets; this often means that carry traders survive turmoil by stampede, their investments gored by severe depreciation. Most of these currencies show steady appreciation for a year or two before their inevitable decline. Carry traders are therefore a nervous, jumpy lot, always poised to withdraw their money if they detect the slightest disturbance in a country. Inevitably, their mere presence creates volatility, and it can blunt the effectiveness of monetary policy, especially in a small and open economy like that of Iceland.

Typically, carry traders had worked at hedge funds and the proprietary desks of banks. In 2005, however, the carry trade quantum jumped when foreign banks began to issue the so-called "glacier bonds," which were denominated in ISK but sold to investors outside the country. The concept behind these bonds, like other Eurobonds issued in high-yielding currencies, was simple. The issuer would buy Icelandic bonds or secure Icelandic interest rates with some kind of a swap contract, then bundle it to issue a new bond denominated in ISK that would be guaranteed by a bank or another party with a high AAA rating. The new bond would earn 2 to 3 percent lower interest than the underlying Icelandic assets, and the issuer would thus receive a fat spread.

About 60 to 70 percent of all glacier bonds issued were arranged by the London branch of the Canadian bank Toronto Dominion (TD), which actively peddled bonds of various high-yielding currencies on both sides of the Atlantic, carrying hefty fees. TD had a very able chief economist of Swiss origin, Beat Siegenthaler. In Iceland, he was known as "Up-Beat" for his bullish stance on the ISK, but he was also one of the most knowledgeable observers of the Icelandic economy.

The economic brass at the CBI maintained that the carry traders were working for, not against, the country by keeping the krona strong and inflation low. Besides, all economic textbooks stated that a currency appreciation should cool down a small open economy by pressing profits in the export sector and directing demand out of the country into imports. Never mind the uncomfortable evidence to the contrary that was becoming all too visible in Iceland by 2005.

The glacier bonds would then be sold to retail clients— Belgian dentists, Italian widows, etc.—who had a very vague idea of what exchange rate risk meant, but who were delighted to receive high interest with AAA rating. The glacier bond issuing began in August of 2005 and became quite ferocious. It seemed that all the "Belgian dentists" and "Italian widows" of Europe were eager to become the beneficiaries of the high Icelandic interest rates. The demand drove the krona up to levels never seen before. The high interest rate policy of the CBI for the sake of inflation targeting became effectively like self-flagellation for the economy and paved the way for the inevitable currency crisis. Ordinary domestic business in Iceland had only two choices: to accept the punishing double-digit domestic interest rates that effectively transferred funds out of the Icelandic economy and into the hands of foreign speculators or just move on to loans in foreign currency available from the banks and thus accept unacceptable currency risk. Either way, they were in trouble, since five years after the hiking cycle began in 2004, the CBI policy rate is still above 10 percent. During these years of high interest the balance of the foreign speculative position within the Icelandic financial system continued to grow. Sooner or later these speculators would try to escape en masse through the narrow corridor of the currency market, sparking a crisis.

⇥ THE HEDGE FUND ATTACK ⇤

Hedge funds, like wolves, hunt for yield in packs. The force of numbers increases the chances for their trading strategy's success, especially in smaller markets. With a relatively miniscule economy and banks that are large compared with the country but small in relation to international counterparts, it is no surprise that Iceland was perceived as easy quarry. Its financial system was sufficiently contained to be susceptible to an attack from even a handful of hedge funds, in the wake of any bad news.

While the coordinated shorting of the ISK in 2006 was but one of several such episodes Iceland endured in the span of a few years, it was the best documented. Several fund managers in the pack boasted freely about their accomplishments instead of adhering to the usual code of secrecy. Taking down a whole country is more gratifying to the ego, apparently, than taking down a mere corporation.

The action began inside an informal club of about 50 macro hedge funds that organized through Drobny Global Advisors, a research firm based in Manhattan Beach, California. Drobny is run by strategists Andres Drobny and Steven Drobny (no relation). The membership fee for tapping their exclusive circle is upward of $50,000, for which members receive the *Drobny Global Monitor*, a market strategy newsletter that facilitates the exchange of trading ideas. The club holds semiannual meetings or retreats, which feature appearances by intellectual glitterati such as Nouriel Roubini, Niall Ferguson, and Steven Pinker. Individual hedge fund managers also present their trading strategies; the best is given the Drobny Award for "favorite trade."

The impetus for shorting the ISK seems to have come from Jim Leitner, manager of the New Jersey–based Falcon Family Fund. Leitner worked as a currency trader for several major U.S. banks and has decades of experience as a hedge fund manager. He has invested all around the globe in various instruments, such as stocks of Turkish glass-makers, of Serbian construction businesses, and fertilizer companies in Taiwan. The relationship between Leitner and the two Drobnys appears to have been a close one. Leitner had appeared publicly on numerous occasions praising and recommending the club to other managers, and he was also interviewed for *Inside the House of Money*, a book on hedge funds written by Steven Drobny in 2006. In that book, Leitner claims that since he founded the Falcon Family Fund in 1997, he has been able to deliver a 30 percent annual return and has "harvested about $2 billion from the markets" during his career as a hedge fund manager.

Leitner is well acquainted with Iceland. He first visited the country in 1989 and maintained his connections to the country's financial market. He owned about a 1–2% stake in investment bank Straumur-Burdaras and sat on its board. In 2003, he led the Drobnite funds into Iceland to buy inflation-index-linked housing bonds, which had a major impact on the market at the time. Leitner and the Drobnys often refer to that trade in the U.S. press as an example of their club's ingenuity. "Where else would you hear about indexed linked housing bonds from Iceland?" wrote John Bonaccolta (in the Dow Jones Newswire, September 22, 2003). "This was just one idea that came out of the last Drobny Global Conference, where clients sat around and discussed the best trade ideas in an informal setting."

In early February 2006, Leitner sent out an e-mail suggesting that the Drobnites go short against the krona and other high-yielding currencies. The krona was overvalued and ripe for correction, as was the New Zealand dollar. The time of quantitative easing from the major central banks, such as the Bank of Japan, was coming to a halt. It seemed likely that traditional carry trade investors would soon get cold feet and stampede. This would pound the ISK downward.

The Drobnites took his advice and soon they were in luck—whether they made it themselves or not. The New Zealand dollar began to slide; on February 21, Fitch Ratings changed the outlook on Iceland from "stable" to "negative," citing a "material deterioration" in macroeconomic risk indicators and slack fiscal policy. The report mentioned specifically that private sector borrowing had trebled to three times Iceland's GDP in the past three years, and that the current account deficit accounted for 15 percent of its economy. The ISK instantly shed 7.5 percent of its value and would fall 20 to 25 percent over the next two months. The Icelandic stock index, ICEX also took a hit.

Another Drobny member, Hugh Hendry, manager of Eclectica Asset Management, sent out a monthly report on March 31, 2006, in which he stated that he had 75 percent of his fund's assets "short carry, most notably against the Icelandic Krona and the New Zealand dollar." More specifically, about 25 percent of his fund was tied in short position against the ISK. For variety's sake, perhaps, 12 percent of his fund was invested in the stock of British music company EMI!

Hendry told the *British Times* the following summer that he wanted to be "known as the man who bankrupted Iceland." He went so far as to compare himself to his hero, George Soros, whose bets helped to force the pound out of the EMS fixed exchange rate mechanism in the 1990s. In the same interview Hendry claimed that he was "a Joan of Arc–type manager; I hear voices in my head."

Whether those voices told him to short Iceland is unclear. What is certain is that at the next Drobny event, held in Santa Monica, California, that April, Leitner garnered the favorite trade award for shorting the ISK. The group's next event was held in Iceland, on October 12–13; CBI's chief economist received a special invitation and was granted his own Drobny Award, in what seems to have been a mock ceremony, "for best defense of currency."

In the meantime, the situation in the CDS market was deteriorating into crisis. A number of critical reports had helped to widen the spread on all the Icelandic banks up to about 50 to 60 basis points over Libor. But the most original and best—albeit the most scathing—credit report on the Icelandic banks was published by Merrill Lynch on March 7, 2006, and titled "Icelandic Banks—Not What You Are Thinking." It was written by analyst Richard Thomas and must have been a career highlight, both in terms of prestige and profit. Thomas raised again the concerns about the dependence on wholesale funding, short maturity profile, and private equity positions of the Icelandic banks. But he also argued that Iceland's banks were more comparable with those in emerging markets rather than in other European countries. This was not because the Icelandic banks, as such, were un-European in character, but rather because the nation's systemic financial risks were typical of still-maturing countries.

Once again, the thinking behind the theory was straightforward. The business community in an emerging market is dominated by the small, elite ownership of its largest corporations and banks. Cross ownership and cross lending are common and risk is therefore systemic. Iceland's business community was cross connected in precisely this way, given its tiny population and the lack of foreign equity investment. All three banks were in the same boat; the potential for a systematic collapse was high, and similar to the threats faced by emerging-market economies. Thomas further argued that the rating agencies had not taken this systemic risk into account, and that the rating of the Icelandic banks was therefore too high. His blunt recommendation was to short the CDS of the Icelandic banks.

The Thomas report had profound and immediate influence over the London financial community's outlook on Iceland. It was published on a Tuesday, when the CDS spread of Kaupthing was 63 basis points above Libor; by Friday, the spread had reached 80, and it jumped to about 100 on the following Monday before narrowing to about 70 to 80, where it remained for several weeks. This was a wider spread on Kaupthing with an A1 rating than that of Banca Popolare Italiana (rated BBB-plus by Moody's), which was about to produce a fully audited yearly account under new management after its former CEO had been imprisoned for fraud. Of course, in the global crisis two to three years later, most sovereigns of Europe would see their CDS spread rise above 100 basis points.

Merrill Lynch, publisher of the Thomas report, was incidentally one of the prime brokers of the Petroleum Fund of Norway; it is impossible to determine how active PFN was in the trading that followed the report's release. What is clear is that a pack of hedge funds was shorting the bonds of Icelandic banks through the CDS market. They were even able to short the bonds of the Icelandic government, even though it was debt free and had almost no issues outstanding! This was what Morgan Stanley Fixed Income Research, on March 13, called "trading on rumor and innuendo rather than fundamentals" and what JP Morgan's fixed income department, on March 24, described as "people with strong negative opinions exercising their views." Indeed, during March and April of 2006 the issues of Kaupthing were the most traded corporate bond in Europe.

There were also countless requests from the hedge funds to short the Icelandic stock market, especially the banks. However, shorting equities requires borrowing them from stockholders; almost all ICEX stock was in Icelandic hands and unavailable to the stymied hedge funds. However, it is very likely that the Drobnites were joined by a number of other hedge funds in their trade in the currency market as the crisis progressed, including one of George Soros's hedge funds.

THE ICELANDIC COUNTERATTACK

With the ISK in free fall and the CDS spread of the banks touching 100 basis points, Iceland was now subject to an international media feeding frenzy. News reports with garish headlines—"Iceland Melting," "Icelandic Eruption," "Hot Lava," "Geyser Crisis"—were being published daily. Overwhelmed by the unprecedented attention, fearful as their currency depreciated sharply, Icelanders wondered if all the apocalyptic predictions could be true. Foreigners had never cared what happened inside their country before, and its sudden infamy, both bewildering and invasive, was impossible to banish from their minds. Credit reports from the UK went straight into the public domain and generated heated discussions in the national media. Initially, the public faulted the banks for having brought trouble to the country with their foreign expansion. The government, keen on eluding responsibility for the bad news, did little to take the banks off the hook.

On March 21, a new player emerged when the Danske Bank, riding the coattails of London credit reports, published its sole report to date on the Icelandic economy. Circumstances surrounding the publication were peculiar, to say the least. Just prior to the release, Danske Bank closed all lines to Iceland, including the CBI, and refused all trading in the Icelandic krona; this meant that, in effect, the bank disallowed its clients trade in Icelandic assets while simultaneously conducting "impartial" research on the country.

In truth, Danske Bank seemed to be eager to step into the limelight and garner international exposure for its research team by reporting on the hot topic of the day. The general conclusion of the report was that Iceland, frozen out of the international capital market, was going down in a singular financial crisis with a sharp output contraction. However, since Iceland was so small, its downfall would have little or no impact on the outside world, except, perhaps, that the Scandinavians could acquire assets held by Icelandic companies abroad at fire sale prices.

The Danske Bank analysts achieved their goal of becoming prominent Icelandic commentators on international newswires, and modesty was not one of their virtues. They also became cheerleaders for the hedge funds whether that was conscious or not. They boasted that their words could move the ISK, joked about the Russian mafia in Iceland, and were sure to tease out the worst-case scenario from every internal development. This stirred up great resentment in the Icelandic financial community. It suspected that Danske Bank was hell-bent on making their forecast a self-fulfilling prophecy, since the continuing devaluation of the ISK was pushing the inflation rate above 8 percent and destabilizing the system.

Simultaneously, Iceland was receiving withering criticism in the Danish media, some of it laced with outright prejudice. Danish publications, among other things, warned their countrymen not to take work in any enterprise owned by an Icelandic citizen. The negativity spread to other Scandinavian countries, and bogus claims, such as that Icelandic banks were engaging in rackets or money laundering for the Russian mafia, became commonplace.

The backlash was quick and furious. Icelanders felt belittled and talked down to by their Scandinavian cousins and took it very personally—especially when the vituperation came from Danes. The public mood shifted on the side of the banks. Sensing that they were being railroaded, with hedge funds on one side and an international yellow press on the other, the Icelanders closed ranks and planned a counterattack.

On April 20, Danske Bank analysts published a one-page note titled "ISK Trouble Set to Continue." They stated that the economy was collapsing faster than they had forecast, and strongly recommended shorting of the Icelandic krona. The note was preceded by a sell-off in the Icelandic currency market, as Scandinavian banks moved in for the kill and joined the hedge funds in selling down the ISK. April 20 was a Thursday, and the first day of summer in Iceland, a traditional holiday; the currency market was closed in observance. The day was used to pool together whatever foreign currency the Icelandic private sector possessed in the banks, fishing firms, and pension and investment funds, and to organize a defense of the ISK.

On Friday, April 21, when the currency market opened again, the ISK went instantly into free fall—but only for the first two hours. Then, suddenly, foreign currency poured into the market and fueled a rebound. In the next hours, the hedge funds made repeated attacks on the currency, turning volumes after volumes of sales offers for the ISK, but each one was met. In a one-day market turnover that equaled 7 percent of Iceland's GDP, the ISK held firm and closed at its opening value.

This was a major reversal after two months of almost continuous losses. Trading would remain at accelerated levels for the remainder of the month—the turnover in April 2006 equaled 50 percent of Iceland's GDP—but the ISK steadied and the currency crisis fizzled out. The Scandinavian banks were beaten back with heavy losses and the Drobny hedge funds, one by one, began to take profit and drop out of the market.

The CDS market was the next area of concern. The prime minister of Iceland filed a complaint with his colleague in Norway that addressed the CDS shorts the Petroleum Fund of Norway had amassed against the Icelandic banks, even though PFN did not actually own any bonds issued by the banks. The Norwegian government intervened and PFN was ordered to unwind all its positions; along the way, Havik lost his job.

The third phase of the counterattack was a concerted effort to inform the world that Iceland had not melted. To this end, the Icelandic Chamber of Commerce contracted Frederic Mishkin, then a professor at Columbia, to write a report on the Icelandic economy as a coauthor with an Icelandic professor, Tryggvi Thor Herbertsson. The report, published on May 2, gave the Icelandic economy and financial system a clean bill of health. Indeed, the report became a media sensation, and Mishkin and Herbertsson went on to present it in lectures in the major financial capitals.

Just ten days later, Morgan Stanley recommended that their clients go long in the CDS market for the Icelandic banks, stating that the Mishkin report had "convinced us that Iceland does not display meltdown characteristics nor that it could be forced into one by market fear/intent." The CDS narrowed by 20 basis points in the next two weeks.

Richard Thomas of Merrill Lynch would respond to the Mishkin report in a private e-mail sent to Kaupthing's employee. He said that he did not find the report "too convincing," and that "the numerous typos suggest it was not prepared by a native English speaker!!"

By late May, the Geyser crisis was over. The media, referencing "Iceland fatigue," at last turned its attention elsewhere. The defense had succeeded. The Mishkin report would remain a handy tool for when the banks turned toward the United States for funding.

⊰ LESSONS—HEEDED AND UNHEEDED ⊱

What made the Geyser crisis a distinctive event was the intensity with which the entire world focused on a single, tiny dot on the financial map, even for two months. Iceland was feared to be the canary in the coal mine. As the smallest independent currency region in the world, the island had the "smallest lungs," and was expected to faint when liquidity became scarce and to sound an early warning for the rest of the world. This expectation, in the end, was both right and wrong. Iceland did not collapse in 2006, because the global liquidity glut continued for one more year. But in the end, Iceland did in fact become an early warning epicenter.

If the Danske Bank analysts had been correct in claiming that the Icelandic economy was a deviation, a crisis without global significance, it probably would have been the first time a whole country was taken down by hedge funds. Two years later, however, many other nations would be facing precisely the same problems, created by their own oversized banking systems and independent currencies. Denmark, for instance, suffered the collapse of a larger housing bubble than that of Iceland, and it also became the first country in Europe to enter into recession, in the second quarter of 2008.

Moreover, the problems created by the hedge fund attacks would be replayed in the U.S. banking crisis of 2008, during which Bear Sterns, Lehman Brothers, AIG, and other institutions were taken down by bear raids in which the shorting of stocks and practice of CDS trading amplified and reinforced each other. Not surprisingly, there is now a growing demand in the United States to regulate the CDS market and ban "naked" credit-default swap trading. As much as 80 percent of the credit-default swap market is traded by investors who don't own the underlying bonds. In Europe, major financial institutions have yielded to political pressures and founded clearinghouses, and have agreed to increased oversight of the over-the-counter CDS market to improve transparency amid the credit crisis.

In hindsight, it does not seem that the Icelandic government took many lessons from this crisis; certainly preparations against future threats were insufficient. The foreign currency reserves of the CBI were around EUR 1 billion during the Geyser crisis, an amount roughly equivalent to the total turnover on the Icelandic currency market on April 21. In other words, the foreign reserves were sufficient to defend ISK against hedge fund attacks for a day or two.

CBI did double its reserves with a new bond issue in the autumn of 2006. But that did not fundamentally preclude the government's foreign currency holdings from being far below what was needed to ensure the liquidity of its currency area, or even give the appearance that reserves would be sufficient in a time of crisis.

By contrast, the Icelandic banks took the credit reports very seriously. In the ensuing months they would attempt to mend their ways by diversifying their funding structure and extending the maturity profile of their debt. Kaupthing steered clear of the European MTN market and issued bonds in Japan, Canada, Mexico, Australia, and the United States. The banks would also unwind many of their private equity positions and implement stronger guidelines for their proprietary trading desks. Kaupthing would also dissolve their cross shareholdings. The banks in general embraced transparency and disclosure and improved communications with the credit community.

Many in the banking community viewed the crisis of 2006 as a necessary evil, as a catalyst for reforms that would make them stronger and better. What they failed to grasp was that the virtuous cycle of risk diversification through foreign acquisitions had been reversed during the crisis and could not be turned back around. Instead of becoming more "international" by acquiring foreign banking assets, they simply became larger and larger regional banks, since every foreign asset they touched became, instantly, "Icelandic," and classified as part of the indigenous financial system.

Ben Ashby, fixed income analyst for JP Morgan, drew the following conclusions on March 24, 2006:

Interesting thing statistics. Obviously as the Icelanders have expanded abroad they have bought more overseas assets, in the form of other financial institutions. By definition, financial institutions have leveraged balance sheets. Obviously as purchases by Icelandic-domiciled firms these get aggregated to become "Icelandic" overseas obligations— even though some of these businesses have previously had nothing to do with Iceland. We would imagine that if Scotland ever goes independent then RBS and HBOS would have a rather similar effect on Scotland's GDP. Or perhaps closer to home just the City of Westminster or more specifically Curzon Street and Berkeley Square on a standalone basis relative to the rest of London. What we do see as an issue is that when these firms do buy anything overseas quite often it will get reclassified to Icelandic risk by certain financial institutions' risk departments. Obviously, banks tend to have a finite level of single country or name exposure they are willing to take. We think that there is a possibility that while the firm may be diversified, certain counterparties may be increasingly unwilling to take Icelandic risk.

This would, in the end, prove to be a prescient description of the downfall of Icelandic banking.

The British Credit Reports that were critical of Iceland were correct in many respects. Their main point was that the Icelandic banks, given their business model and the lack of support from their central bank and government, would have to pay a higher risk premium than banks from other countries that had the same rating. This was indeed the case after the dust settled in the summer of 2006: the Icelandic banks' CDS spread stabilized, but at a level 30 to 40 basis points higher than banks with a similar rating. The Icelanders argued that their estate was not fundamentally different from that of the UK, Ireland, Switzerland, and Denmark, despite that some figures were skewed. When the global financial crisis struck in 2007, it turned out that both sides were right, although neither one drew the correct lesson from the affair.

CHAPTER 5

LIVING IN A BUBBLE

BEING HANNES SMÁRASON ⊱

On New Year's Eve 2006, Icelanders sat down after their traditional festive dinners to watch the "New Year's Skit" on state television. A parody of the passing year's events, the Skit was a national institution on par with the New Year's fireworks at midnight. This year the memorable joke turned on a man named Hannes Snorrason, an average Joe who was hounded in his daily life with comments like "Hannes Snorrason, yes, sounds almost like Hannes *Smárason* except you are missing something," or more simply, "Why can't you be more like Hannes *Smárason?*"

Icelanders found the plight of this average Joe, with a name too similar to a national luminary's, uproarious. But the joke was on the real man with the name Hannes Smárason—*enfant terrible* of the business world, who was either a crazed gambler or a genius depending on whom you asked. In a country still in touch with its egalitarian roots, Smárason's exposure to condemnation and ridicule was inevitable. He was in for more when a song, leaked onto the Internet around the same time, made sport with lyrics such as "you all know my deeds / I am not like the rest on streets / you should all bow to me" and "This is Hannes Smárason here / I only know how to buy and sell."

But there was abundant evidence that Smárason (born in 1967), a distinguished engineering graduate of MIT and a former McKinsey consultant might be enjoying a laugh of his own. In 2004, he had taken control of Icelandair and in less than two years transformed this national airline, with more than 60 years of business history, into a leveraged investment company. Cultural potshots aside, the irrefutable fact was that in its modern guise, the company had made more money under his brief command than it had in its entire prior existence.

Icelandair became an international carrier in the years following World War II by pioneering discount flights between America and Europe and undercutting the price fixing of other European flag carriers. Luxembourg, the only European nation without a flag carrier, was the first (and only, at the outset) to grant landing permits to Icelandair planes; this relationship later influenced Iceland's decision to make its first financial foreign expansion in Luxembourg. The airline had always stashed its summer profits to help tide it over during the slow winter months. When Smárason gained control in 2004, he began to invest the excess in the stock market. He soon was convinced that there was much more money to be made trading stocks than flying customers across the Atlantic. In early 2005, the company was officially designated an investment company and changed its name to FL Group.

In the beginning Smárason had been working with the established business elite—the wife of Geir Haarde, then the minister of finance and the soon to become prime minister, was sitting on the board of the new company. However, midway through the year, the entire board resigned, citing as their reason the management style and bellicose investment tactics of their chairman—Smárason. Their complaints were echoed when the CEO quit in October. Undaunted, Smárason pressed on and named himself the new CEO. He managed to raise a new equity offering, and continued to invest. The equity offering was unusual because stocks in other companies were accepted as payments. Since FL Group traded at a premium book value—a reflection of the market's exuberant belief in Smárason's business acumen—there was an instantaneous "value creation" when FL's premium was added onto the value of stocks booked at market value.

FL Group at the outset kept its focus on the airline industry. An early major purchase had been a stake in EasyJet, the UK discount airline, which was sold at a hefty profit in the midst of the Geyser crisis. That autumn, Smárason divested Icelandair out of FL Group and listed it as a separate company on the Icelandic stock exchange, booking another rich profit. In the final months of 2006, FL acquired a 5.98 percent stake in the AMR Corporation—the U.S. holding company that owned American Airlines—and became the third-largest shareholder in that entity. AMR had shown a profit in the first two quarters of 2006, for the first time in six years, and its stock price had subsequently appreciated 36 percent in the last two quarters, realizing another instant profit for FL. When the numbers were all in, Smárason could boast a 40 percent return on his investments in 2006. It had indeed been his year.

Smárason's achievement received high-profile recognition when "The Market," the business section of the most widely circulated newspaper in Iceland, chose him as businessman of the year for 2006. In an interview that followed this accolade, on December 28, Smárason boasted that he did not need to deal with Icelandic banks anymore: in fact, he said, he *was* the bank now. During the stock market sell-off at the height of the Geyser crisis, he had grabbed a 30 percent stake in Glitnir (formerly Islandsbanki) using a foreign syndicated loan.

FL had been operating like a hedge fund, with active proprietary trading, but its modus operandi was to take large enough stakes in its acquisitions to give it a voice on the companies' boards. That voice exhorted management to undertake "value-adding reforms" and should be loud enough to be heeded. Now focusing on banks, FL bought a stake in the German Commerzbank in 2007. All indicators pointed upward and Hannes Smárason's reputation as a genius grew for a few more months, anyway. When an economic downturn began in the fall of 2007, airlines and banks were among the first casualties and FL Group was hit by a series of margin calls. Smára-son was forced to step down as the CEO in the fall of 2007 and his positions were sold.

A quick rise and precipitous fall: it would not be the last in Iceland.

⇥ THE ICEX FROM DAWN TO DECADENCE ⇤

The years between 1997 and 2007 were a golden decade for the Icelandic stock market and investment banking. The banks went from rags to riches advising their clients on cross-border acquisitions; in the process they aided the creation of a handful of Icelandic-owned multinationals. In this regard, necessity had been the mother of invention. Even after the country opened up to the world, liberated its economy and embraced Thatcherian free market virtues, it still could not attract foreign equity investment in any sector except for industries seeking cheap energy like aluminum smelting. It was not for lack of trying. In 2002, during the final phase of bank privatization, the government approached a number of foreign banks with invitations to take a stake in the two banks in which it retained interest, but the response was tepid at best.

Perhaps Iceland was just too small, unknown, and remote a market? It had the smallest free-floating currency in the world and was a minute, anomalous linguistic area. International financial markets were accustomed to the presence of resident Swedes, Danes, and Norwegians; Icelanders were still a rarity. Iceland just continued to a universe onto itself.

On the other hand, the willingness of foreigners to *lend* money to Iceland on the back of her excellent credit ratings seemed almost bottomless. The country needed scale economics, multinationals, and tasks worthy of its ambitious, foreign-educated workforce. (Many Icelandic students attained their advanced degrees abroad, but most returned home when they were ready to raise a family.) By the same token, the investment banks recognized that the mountain would not come to them and so went to the mountain, creating multinationals in a string of leveraged transactions. They spent the first part of the golden decade building successful companies with real agendas in the world markets. What was more, growth was achieved without a single default by a major Icelandic corporation or the issue of any corporate bonds, despite the huge amount of leverage being used.

By dividing the golden decade into three general phases, we can better understand the rationale that informed the stock market bubble that began to grow in 2005 and the systematic collapse that followed three years later. Those three phases are:

• *The buildup (1997–2000).* This initial phase described the maturation of a young, thin market that had been active only since 1992. During this time, 42 new companies were listed on the stock exchange, bringing the total number up to 75 by 1999 and the total market cap to 100 percent of the GDP. The growth was driven by both privatization and rationalization in the corporate sector. The new listings were companies operating for the most part intramurally, although some were producing for the export markets, particularly fishing companies. A small minority were connected to the dot-com bubble. The benchmark index was comprised of the 15 biggest and most liquid companies (ICEX-15); from 1997 to 1999 it approximately doubled before shedding the gain almost completely in 2000–2001. This phase coincided with the dawn of Icelandic investment banking and represented the first step toward a healthy market economy in Iceland.

• *Internationalization of the stock market (2002–2005).* During this time a number of leading companies became multinationals through leveraged cross-border acquisitions, facilitated by the quickly developing expertise in international investment banking. Most of them mined specialized niches in three oversized industries: health, fishing, and biotech. They facilitated the production and export of "real goods" and, by acquiring foreign companies, they invested in production synergies and market access. Their acquisition targets were bought on low multiples due to generally cheap equity prices. In these years, international policy rates and risk premium both dropped, magnifying returns of leveraged equity investments. The expanding companies followed well-defined strategies and sound business models that in most cases proved successful; they brought extravagant returns to their domestic shareholders and new, well-paying jobs to educated Icelanders.

Kaupthing had been foraying in cross-border investment strategies since 1999 and quickly established its authority; its own expansion was achieved on the backs of successful clients. The ICEX in general was focused on foreign expansion, its growth fueled by a low-dividend payout ratio. Companies bound to the domestic market were subject to a wave of leveraged buyouts generated by the priorities of international players. Dominant shareholders either took these interests private or else were swallowed by larger companies.

At this time, keeping up with the Joneses of Icelandic business meant leveraged equity investments. In 2000 the first company was delisted from the ICEX in a leveraged transaction and there would be more. For example, from 2003 practically all fishing companies were delisted from the ICEX; the number of indexed companies shrunk to 27 by 2005 (from 75 companies in 1999). Simultaneously, the market cap swelled from 60 percent of the GDP to 180 percent as the ICEX index tripled. Now that 70 percent of the revenue of ICEX companies came from abroad, the stock market at last could be described as an international entity. On the other hand, it was still a local concern: foreign investors *still* were not tapping into the ICEX, despite having many internationals to choose from. But from any perspective, investment banking was enjoying its halcyon days. Its dominance placed the ICEX in step with its Scandinavian counterparts, over which large, niche-playing multinationals were also running herd.

• *Fixing on financials (2005–2007).* Near the end of this final phase, financials constituted about 85 percent of the ICEX-15 market cap. Listing an investment company that owned shares in other listed companies, such as the banks, had the peculiar effect of counting real value many times over. Cross-border acquisitions by now were composed mostly of pure equity investments made by holding companies, rather than companies focused on nuts-and-bolts production. Furthermore, Icelanders had run out of qualifying candidates for would-be multinationals. Acquisition targets had jumped in price since all multiples in the international equity market continued appreciation along with the economic boom abroad and leverage ratios increased.

This was, visibly, a time of decadence in the stock market. Investment companies and financial engineering, markets that had grown with the economy at large, were experiencing a bubble and dominating the nest. The ICEX market cap was three times the GDP in mid-2007; wealth effects trickled down and took the form of record sales of champagne and luxury cars. In hindsight, this was the point when rational economic calculations came to a halt. The currency was overvalued, household income was unsustainable, and all valuations were skewed. In their ambition, Icelanders had overreached, setting themselves up for merciless punishment in 2008 in which 90 percent of the stock market value was wiped out.

The stock market exuberance began in 2005 but the fatal wrong turn occurred after the Geyser crisis, when the country's financial market was discovered by the structured credit industry of the United States. CDS spreads of the Icelandic banks remained stubbornly high—30 to 40 points above other banks—even after calm was restored and the crisis had receded from the international newswires. Although Iceland was not yet melting, the London financial community was still demanding an extra risk premium, an especially severe one given the low-spread environment and the lack of new funds coming out of the City. The three Icelandic banks could pass the premium on to their domestic clients, but that option did not exist with foreign clients, who might be lost to banks of other nations. In the end, Icelanders were likely to have been priced out of foreign markets and their expansion would have slowed or ground to a halt. The banks even had to shrink their balance sheets in response to funding pressures.

But fortune's wheel again seemed to turn in Iceland's favor in late 2006, when new demand for Icelandic bond issues arose. These bonds combined high yields with high ratings, which made them ideal building blocks for securitization. They were bundled with other corporate bonds in special purpose entities (SPEs) issuing collateralized debt obligations (CDOs). The risk and return to the end investor depended primarily on how the CDOs and their tranches were defined; the underlying assets had only an indirect effect. It actually seems that the majority of investors never gave much thought to what their CDOs were composed of, beyond the basic information supplied by their rating.

Indeed, a high return with a good rating looked almost like a free lunch. We now know that the debt-securitization market contained a structural flaw that contributed mightily to the current financial and banking crises, especially in the United States: the ability to earn large fees from originating and securitizing loans, coupled with the lack of any residual liability, skewed originators' incentives in favor of loan *volume*, and return rather than quality. This was most evident in the use of the so-called subprime mortgages in structured credit, and it was this practice that, starting in 2006, sucked the Icelandic financial system into the brewing U.S. credit bubble. When the bubble burst a year later, it was at first called the "subprime crisis."

But in 2006, the CDO alchemists were a boon to Iceland. They weaved Icelandic banking bonds and bare CDS contracts into so-called synthetic CDOs. This encouraged financiers to go long against the Icelanders in the CDS market by writing insurances against their default. Thus, the banks' spreads narrowed almost overnight. Simultaneously, the U.S. MTN market opened suddenly to Icelandic banking bonds, prompting all three banks to answer with new issues. The wholesale markets could again be utilized. Out of the blue, foreign credit markets were wide open again, and all the banks rushed forward. The Geyser crisis had, after all, done nothing to curb their desire for growth.

Fortune extended another gift in early 2007, when Moody's upgraded all three banks to a triple A rating, a jump of four or (for

Landsbanki) five notches. This was the product of a new methodology called joint default analysis (JDA), which estimated the likelihood of default on banking bonds as the likelihood of government support for the respective banks. Moody's noted that there had been virtually no bank defaults in the last 30 or 40 years, *in countries with a history of supporting banks.* The JDA was critical to the inflation of the international credit bubble; many banks received rating upgrades with its application, although Iceland's were the most spectacular. Triple As made the banks' bonds all the more attractive to weavers of the CDOs, and credit flowed even more readily.

Moody's responded to explicit and immediate criticism of the Icelandic upgrades in a Q&A it sent out to investors to explain the JDA method. The form pointed out that the three banks represented over 90 percent of domestic deposits and a similar, if not larger, share of domestic loans. Since each individual bank accounted for at least 25 percent of the financial system, Moody's believed that each of them clearly qualified as "too important to fail." Concerning the backup support of the nation's government, the agency maintained that "access to finance will always be available for Iceland—albeit at varying prices. Moreover, adjustments to shocks in advanced economies are made through GDP growth rates and flexible exchange rates, and not by defaulting on debt obligations."

This explanation did not convince the skeptics. Even Kaupthing's CEO publicly voiced doubt about JDA. Just days later, Moody's reversed the upgrades, dropping each bank down three notches, still one or two higher than before JDA was implemented.

⊰ THE RISE OF THE HOLDING COMPANIES ⊱

During the heady recovery of late 2006, fair-weather friends on both sides of the Atlantic bestowed another gift on the owners of Iceland's banks. They were now able to pledge their shares as collateral for direct lending from the large international banks. The shares were kept in holding companies, which originally had been of modest size, but grew in tandem with the continued success of the foreign banking expansion. The holding companies had been leveraged from the very beginning. For example, Samson Holdings, the main owner of Landsbanki, had bought a 48.3 percent share of the bank when the state sought privatization in 2002; the deal included a 30 percent equity ratio with the remaining 70 percent vendor financed.

In the old equalitarian Iceland there was little concentration of wealth; there were no "super rich" to speak of, and the small number of old moneyed families rarely could produce the funds for substantial corporate investment. Thus, the owners of holding companies and architects of the new multinationals depended on leverage at the outset, since so few funds were available. It was not until 2006 that success abroad created substantial equity in the holding companies and world-class wealth for their owners. However, when the opportunity arose that fateful autumn of 2006 the capital gains from the past three years were leveraged anew with new external funding. The holding companies transformed themselves into investment bodies by blowing up their balance sheet.

These new investment entities now pursued ambitious international goals. Their initial forays into foreign stock markets were so profitable as to encourage smaller imitators back home who were funded locally. The lofty expectations for these leveraged stock bets can be inferred, for instance, from the fact that ICEX-listed investment companies were being traded around price to book 1.5, which means, effectively, that the market value of their stock was 50 percent above the market's *already* elevated valuation of their assets. By mid-2007, one-quarter of Icelandic banking's total lending had been done with holding companies with collateral, mostly in equity.

The transition from holding to investment companies is well illustrated by a series of mergers and acquisitions that centered on Exista, the primary owner of Kaupthing.

Exista was founded in 2001 (then under the name Meidur) as a holding vehicle for Kaupthing shares owned by savings and loan institutions, which had owned the majority of the bank since 1985. In 2003, two brothers, Lýdur and Ágúst Gudmundsson, acquired a 55 percent stake in Exista. The Gudmundssons had founded an ICEX-listed company named Bakkavör in 1986 and thus came to be known as the Bakka brothers as their profile widened. They were classic auto-didacts who had built their company from scratch, without any specialized education. In the beginning of their venture, Bakkavör was involved in the processing of roe, the same business Gudmundsson *père* had spun-off from the fishing industry. But the brothers soon transformed their vehicle into a leading producer of fresh convenience foods; they eventually would exit the Icelandic fishing sector altogether. In 1997, they crossed paths with Kaupthing and began their international expansion with a string of leveraged transactions.

The first foreign acquisition was made in France, in 1997, but the Bakka brothers became truly aggressive when they entered the British market in 2000. In 2001, they made the watershed acquisition of the UK-based Katsouris Fresh Foods, a company five times the size of Bakkavör. Four years later they acquired their main British competitor, Geest, which was roughly three or four times the size of their company. By now Bakkavör had become a leading maker of fresh prepared food in the UK. The group's products, made under supermarkets' labels, ranged from ready meals, pizzas, fresh salads, soups and dips, to desserts and ready-to-eat fruit. Although the growth to some extent had been financed with offerings in the Icelandic stock market, the company had similar leverage as a private equity fund. After success in the food business had begun to materialize, the Bakka brothers turned their attention to financials and accumulated a substantial stake in Kaupthing; when they became the leading owners of Exista, the brothers brought along their Kaupthing shares and a 39.6 percent stake in Bakkavör.

Now Exista had become the bank's biggest shareholder, with about a 23 percent stake. The goal here, to ensure stability in the bank's shareholder base, was based on Swedish models, such as Investor AB, which supports Svenska Enskilda Banken, or Industrivärden, which supports Svenska Handelsbanken. By 2005, Exista was ready to succeed as an investment company, and to that end purchased Icelandic National Telecom when it was privatized. By the end of that year, Exista flaunted a balance sheet of EUR 2 billion and a 60 percent equity ratio.

Exista and Kaupthing had had cross ownership from the outset, with the bank owning a 19 percent stake in the company. This served a limited strategic interest for Kaupthing, since under international capital adequacy rules this share was subtracted from its equity base and the shares were carried on the books at original purchase price. During the Geyser crisis, however, Kaupthing was harshly criticized for this practice and the management devised a clever exit strategy. In a September public offering, Exista was listed on the ICEX as an investment company. When Kaupthing paid out its Exista shares as an extra dividend to its shareholders, overnight Exista was endowed with 36,000 new shareholders. For its part, Exista was intent on becoming a "financial service group," with northern Europe as its core market. The plan was to benefit from the strong cash flow between the operating units and the investment arm of the company.

The ideal and best-known model of this practice was Warren Buffett's Berkshire Hathaway. Buffett's company uses the "float" provided by insurance operations (a policyholder's money, which it holds temporarily until claims are paid out) to finance its investments. To this end, Exista acquired an insurance company called VIS (with about 35 percent market share in the Icelandic market) from Kaupthing in May 2006. In early 2007, Exista used direct foreign financing to build up a 20 percent stake in a Finnish insurance company, Sampo, and a 8 to 9 percent stake in a Norwegian investment company, Storebrand (Kaupthing at that time already held a 20 percent stake in Storebrand). The plan, clearly, was to employ the Berkshire Hathaway model throughout Scandinavia by acquiring insurance companies, with one crucial difference. Buffett sternly warns against leverage; leverage had become Exista's middle name. By midyear 2007, its balance sheet had swelled to EUR 7.7 billion—and 37 percent equity ratio.

Exista was the largest, most sophisticated Icelandic investment company to emerge in the stock boom, but there were many others. While only the top players could solicit direct foreign financing, all exploited tax incentives that made the formation of a holding company very attractive indeed. Some holding companies were course organized around business involved in real production but others, from the outset, had been little more than stock trading vehicles, but by 2005 it had become common for traditional businesses to use their excess cash flow for equity investment and even to leverage their operational assets. This was the case with Smárason's FL Group and with many fishing companies as well. The latter were accustomed to financing themselves in the foreign currencies in which they received income or conducted other hedging activities. But most investment companies were in fact the overhauled holding company of some traditional Icelandic business that, after the unprecedented market growth, now held substantial assets. The owners, seduced by the temptation to leverage, would acquire another company or just buy listed shares.

The holding company structure, then, also contributed to the ICEX bubble; in fact, almost the whole financial system had now become a derivative of the successful foreign expansion of Iceland's three banks. The Savings Bank of Reykjavik (SPRON) was an extreme example of this. In the summer of 2007, its market capitalization was ISK 120 billion ($2 billion at the prevailing exchange rate), which was equal to three times the book value of equity. The SPRON had approximately 20,000 customers. Its main asset was a share in Exista, which traded at 1.6 book value of equity. The main asset of Exista, meanwhile, was Kaupthing, which traded at up to two times equity. The owners of shares in the innocuous-sounding Reykjavik Savings Bank were therefore holding incestuous equity of Kaupthing at almost ten times book value.

Lending against the value of a listed equity does not have to carry a higher risk than, say, lending against the value of a house, if the underlying stock can be sold in a liquid market on short notice. If that is the case, the bank can just liquidize the position by placing a margin call on the loan and recover the funds. The Icelandic banks made the loans to the holding companies based on what they considered to be a comfortable equity buffer, over 50 percent coverage. Some of the companies had engaged in a leveraged buyout along the way and kept what they considered to be a long-term holding of unlisted equity; most held marketable assets and/or listed stocks, which presumably could be sold after a margin call to repay the loan. Iceland was not unique in this area, since the most profitable and fastest-growing segment of banking on both sides of the Atlantic was loans to hedge funds or investment companies.

What *was* unusual was the precarious liquidity of the ICEX. Despite many Icelandic companies having foreign revenues, the country's equity market was in essence its own universe, with almost no foreign ownership. A bank could in most cases easily liquidate its holding company's client portfolio through a margin call, sell it in the market, and recover its loan. However, the portfolios of all the bank's clients were very similar and therefore highly correlated. That included the bank's most important customers, owners, and managers. If the need arose, liquidating the whole system in an orderly fashion proved impossible. This, like much else, worked well until stock markets the world over found themselves in a systemic liquidity crisis after August 2007. Both the banks and the holding companies were rendered nearly illiquid by the shock. At the same time, the holding companies were monitored relentlessly by foreign short traders and hedge funds. These predators would jump on any rumor about an immediate sale of foreign holdings and short the company's main assets, effectively blocking its exit. Exista, for one, was a sitting duck in this game. Shorting its three main listed assets brought down the equity ratio and, the hedge funds hoped, would trigger a margin call and a forced sale. Which it eventually did.

⊰ THE BANKS AND THEIR OWNERS ⊱

All the while, Icelandic bankers were ambivalent about the investment companies souping up on their own by obtaining loan financing directly from foreign banks. Some were pleased to reduce risk in the home financial system by transferring credit risk to foreign banks and reducing cross lending. In some cases, such as Kaupthing and Exista, the bank goaded the investment company into more outward reach. But there were general worries about loose cannons cornering power through foreign leverage, the most infamous of these cannons being Hannes Smárason and his FL Group.

As it turned out, the balance sheet enlargement of these investment companies with direct foreign funding created an extra layer of foreign leverage on the value of the banks' stock prices, to the grave detriment of the Icelandic financial system. The inflated sheets crumpled as soon as the foreign banks withdrew their support in response to the crisis inside the international financial markets. Their sheer weight was almost enough to crush the banks.

However in 2006–2007, the aggressive, leveraged giants remained wonderful banking clients, who created new fees in both capital markets and investment bank divisions. They frequently established their own hedge-fund-type proprietary trading arms for short-term position taking as well as strategic long-term positions in selected companies. Some companies even co-invested with the banks in selected projects. Furthermore, a bigger owner could better support the continued growth of the banks with new equity. The relations had gone far beyond the old model of client-partner: this was a symbiotic relationship, or even a strategic alliance.

Inside the Exista-Kaupthing combine, no one doubted that Sigurdur Einarsson and his minions were in charge; Exista was Kaupthing's creation. Once, a major shareholder told Einarsson he was considering the sale of his share to another major Icelandic investor. "Never mind" said Einarsson. "He will never have any say about this bank, not more than you have."

At Landsbanki, the shareholder-management relations skewed in favor of the former, since a single group held a nearly 50 percent stake and had invited the management into their bank. The structure was further complicated by the fact that the owners were active investors, who had come to own a multitude of investment companies as well as Straumur-Burdarás, another investment bank, and all these pieces interacted. What was more, Landsbanki was run by two CEOs who reputedly clashed with each other. One, Sigurjón Árnason, had been recruited with a cadre of loyal followers from Bunadarbanki. He had unquestioned control of the bank and his independence enhanced his credibility outside the bank. His counterpart, Halldór Kristjánsson (born in 1955), had acted as CEO prior to the privatization; his retention was seen as a means to keep a lid on Árnason but it also had political overtones, as will be discussed in Chapter 6.

Islandsbanki traveled the rockiest road during this time, since instead of fostering an investment company it basically was taken over by one. In the process, it was transformed from the most risk-averse bank into the biggest risk-taker. Islandsbanki, since 1989 the only continuously private bank, arguably had the best retail operations in the country in terms of its branch network and corporate loan portfolio. But despite strenuous efforts, it could never gain traction in the investment banking business. Its CEO was Bjarni Ármansson (born 1968), who had worked for Kaupthing from 1992 to 1997 before becoming CEO of the government-owned corporate bank FBA, established in January 1998. FBA merged with Islandsbanki the following year and Ármansson transferred his title to the new bank.

Ármansson was a charismatic and able manager, with an approach to funding and private equity that was conservative by market standards. He was an appealing personality who embroidered in his spare time and ran in highly publicized marathons sponsored by his bank. But for some reason, Islandsbanki still could not fly as an investment banking operation. It might have been that, unlike Einarsson and Árnason, Ármansson never built a stable management team around him; some said this was because he saw able, ambitious employees as threats rather than assets. But he also suffered from the power strug-gles and disunity of the major owners, which so undermined his own position that he earned the nickname "the Survivalist" in honor of the tap-dancing he managed on top of his shifting shareholder base. Islandsbanki's owners were typically the traditional, old-money, over-whelmingly risk-averse elite; these were not the people to create a strategic partnership via the formation of an aggressive investment company. Islandsbanki had, though, been a pioneer in fostering investment companies when it established Straumur, originally an equity fund founded in 1986 which became a listed investment com-pany in 2001. However, in 2003–2004 Landsbanki owners were able to snatch the fund from Islandsbanki and upgrade it into an invest-ment bank under the name Straumur-Burdarass in 2005.

However, even these cautious actors could see that their retail bank's future was threatened by the prowling presence of the Landsbanki and Kaupthing. Islandsbanki lost employees and clients after its com-petitors were privatized, and it fended off a hostile takeover attempt by Landsbanki in 2004. Outward growth was essential to survival. Ármansson aspired to turn Islandsbanki into an Icelandic-Norwegian commercial bank with a special emphasis on the marine sector and renewable energy. When he acquired two regional Norwegian banks in 2004—Kreditbanken, which concentrated on the seafood sector, and BN, a specialist in long-term mortgages—Islandsbanki became the sole Icelandic bank to make a foray into foreign retail operations. This, then, was to become the soil in which its investment banking operations would take root in Norway. There was even a change of name: the bank was now called Glitnir, a more Pan-Scandinavian name derived, not surprisingly, from Old Norse mythology.

Glitnir's retail approach carried far less risk, a fact revealed during the Geyser crisis, when its CDS spread was far below that of Kaupthing and Landsbanki. At last, it seemed to have gained a com-petitive edge. Bjarni Ármansson, previously criticized for his conser-vatism, now stood vindicated in the wake of the crisis. But the market's appreciation was truncated when new U.S. funding sources opened up in the fall of 2006 and investment banking enjoyed its resurgence. Conventional wisdom declared that "no foreign bank has ever made money in Norway," and Glitnir ultimately was unable to contradict that claim. Its Norwegian operations, while not disastrous, did not meet anticipated returns or create a foothold in the corporate market.

It was at this uncertain moment that Hannes Smárason's FL Group took a 30 percent stake in Glitnir. The stake increased in 2007 when FL partnered with Baugur Group, a retail giant. With two leveraged investment companies for owners, the shift in Glitnir's overall strategy was obvious and immediate. The bank jumped into two large deals in the fall of 2006: a takeover of the House of Fraser by Baugur and the underwriting for the sale of Icelandair by FL. To bulk up its capital market operations, it acquired Scandinavian brokerages and investment banking units at very high multiples. Glitnir, too, was now an aggressive investment bank, a fact treated with some skepticism, most notably by Richard Thomas, the credit analyst for Merrill Lynch. The Icelandic financial regulators were also quite skeptical about the new owners of the bank, but the precedent set by the sale of Landsbanki to a leveraged holding company in 2003 made it difficult to act, lest the move be seen as discriminatory. Nevertheless, the Icelandic FSA barred the two investment groups from holding more than 30 percent in the bank, to their great annoyance.

As for Ármansson, by April 2007 his new masters had accumulated sufficient shares to fire him. The new CEO, Lárus Welding (born in 1976), was eight years junior to Ármansson, a fact that did not send a message of independence from owners or experience from the helm.

⇥ THE RISE OF A ROCK STAR ⇤

Baugur Group, a rather mysterious entity, is key to understanding the puzzle of owner-management relations inside the Icelandic banks. The owner and manager was Jón Ásgeir Jóhannesson (born in 1968). He began building his business empire at age 21, when he opened a discount supermarket, Bónus, in Reykjavik's docklands with his sister and father. Jóhannesson *père*, a straight-talking, popular man, had not enjoyed much success in business up to that time. Jóhannesson *fils* didn't have his father's folksy charm or way with words and was an indifferent student, but he was an incredibly determined, driven entrepreneur. It took him just five years to modernize the entire Icelandic food market by streamlining supply networks; along the way Bónus became the country's largest food retailer. When Bónus acquired the largest retail brand, Hagkaup, the new entity was named Baugur (Kaupthing and FBA were advisors to this takeover and, a year later, underwrote Baugur's IPO when it was listed on the ICEX).

Having gathered a healthy market share at home, Jóhannesson was ready to expand abroad. He first targeted the United States in 2000 with a retail advisor, Jim Schafer, who had previously worked at Walmart, buying a bankrupt chain of discount stores. The venture was a dismal failure that ended in bitter strife with Schafer. Jon Ásgeir later described the affair as an expensive business school. An advance into London proved far more successful. By 2001, Baugur, cooperating with Kaupthing and other Icelandic banks, had built a 20 percent stake in Arcadia, a UK retail chain. Baugur attempted a takeover the next year and was rebuffed, but when another company successfully absorbed Arcadia soon after, the Icelanders cashed in £100 million. This windfall made Baugur a major player in the UK retail market. Ultimately, it took stakes or full ownership in a pool of businesses that employed over 65,000 and grossed over 10 billion in 3,800 stores. By now, the British press was referring to Baugur as an archetypal Viking raider—it wasn't just Icelanders who resurrected history.

Jóhannesson went to great lengths to burnish his swashbuckling image. He dressed like a rock star in black suits. The Danish media made fun of the Bundesliga (the German soccer league) hairstyle (his hair falls to his shoulders). His dislike of paperwork and adherence to one-page management were notorious: he didn't want to be flooded with information, he wanted only the essential details and wanted them "quickly." He delisted Baugur from ICEX in 2003, compounding his company's mystique with a public blackout of its balance sheet and income statements. But the Icelanders continued to receive regular updates on the man himself as he took over more UK retail stores, roared about in race cars in Monte Carlo, or partied on his yacht in the Mediterranean. At home and abroad, he became the poster boy for the new dawning of the Viking age or, for those who couldn't swallow the macho act, the descent into crass materialism. There was little doubt about Jóhannesson's self-image— he kept a 10-foot statue of a Viking, armed with a sword and electric guitar, in the lobby of Baugur's London headquarters—and perhaps he missed the irony of his attitude. There was even a swaggering element to his choice of investments, and particularly his purchase of Danish national treasures such as the Magazin du Nord, an historic department store, which annoyed locals to no end.

But business remained a going concern beneath the *opera buffa* persona. The aim behind Jóhannesson's success had been to create a holding company or private equity fund that would carry relatively little debt along with stakes in retail chains obtained in leveraged buyouts. Quite often these would be management-leveraged buyouts that Baugur assisted. If the chain was not leveraged upon purchase, then it would simply take on more loans and pay its owner a dividend. However it ended up under Baugur's umbrella, the chain's management soon had overhanging debt that demanded continued success to keep up with it. The managers ultimately became a very driven lot and in many cases Baugur's stewardship was to produce operational improvements.

Baugur was, after all, something of a Kaupthing creation like most other successful multinationals and the two powerhouses had cooperated closely, especially in the early phase of the invasion into Britain, when Kaupthing actually owned a 20 percent stake in Baugur (that stake was sold in 2006). By 2002, Jóhannesson was successful enough to be wooed by foreign banks, such as the Royal Bank of Scotland, HBOS, Barclays, and Deutsche Bank, all of which cooperated with him in specific deals. When it came to Baugur's funding, an Icelandic bank stood by the equity taps, although not always the *same* banks. He had no trouble finding new partners, as wannabe investment banks considered him the man who could provide access to exclusive clubs in London's financial community. When Kaupthing began to apply the brakes on its lending in 2002–2003, Jóhannesson became cozy with Landsbanki; when they tightened the screws, he bought into Glitnir. When he reached lending limits with this source, he moved on to savings banks and issued corporate bonds directly into the Icelandic financial market. With each new partnership, the leverage and multiples increased along with the new acquisitions to the empire. By the end, it was rumored that Jóhannesson and companies connected to him owed what amounted to between *70 and 80 percent* of the nation's GDP.

Every empire reaches a point where the center gives. It is clear that Jóhannesson, like most of his countrymen, had lost his edge around 2005. His gifts for retail and wealth creation on the UK's High Street were undeniable, but he suffered from an ambition that seemed to have no limits. He had many shops—too many—in Britain and real estate in Sweden and Denmark; he tried to establish a free Danish newspaper, a media conglomerate, a phone company, an Icelandic bank, and, last but not least, a partnership with the ubiquitous Hannes Smárason. Jóhannesson, the man who made his fortune by shaking down sleepy corporate conglomerates in Iceland with his lean, no-frills discount stores was now a bloated conglomerate himself. It is likely that by 2007 he retained little oversight of his empire; he had become surprisingly tolerant of incompetence in his managers.

Jón Ásgeir Jóhannesson is the prime example of the players who made and ultimately broke Iceland. He was a self-made businessman of humble beginnings. He came of age in the newly liberalized Icelandic economy and made something out of nothing with little more than wit, work, and daring. But, like many others of lower profile, he fell prey to overbearing self-confidence, reached for the moon, and lost nearly everything for his efforts.

⊰ THE ABORTED LANDING ⊱

Icelandic economists in the summer of 2006 were in general predicting a downturn. The high jinks in the currency crisis had led to a drop in private consumption and consumer confidence. Since construction on the two aluminum smelters and associated power plants was set to wrap in 2007, investment was also facing decline. It seemed clear that with a cooling economy and lower domestic demand the macro imbalances would correct themselves and the current account deficit, which reached 15 percent of the GDP in 2005, would begin to narrow.

There was ample supportive data for this conclusion. Private consumption had grown at a rate of 10 to 15 percent through 2005 and the 2006 quarters that preceded in the Geyser crisis. In the aftermath, growth slowed to zero, and by the first quarter of 2007 it was in the negative, with households spending 1.4 percent less than they had a year before.

Having grown about 19 percent between 2003 and 2005 (15 percent in per capita terms), the economy was long past the boiling point. With unemployment below 1 percent and the central bank policy rate at 14 percent, there was little chance of squeezing out more growth. These conditions were mitigated, however, by Iceland's now being plugged into the global market. Demand for labor and capital in the overheated economy created its own supply abroad, so the landing was aborted after the winter of 2006–2007 and the upward economic trajectory was restored and extended. Overheated or not, the economy grew an additional 10 percent (5 percent in output per capita) in the next two years. At its apex, Iceland was probably coming close to being the richest nation on earth in terms of per capita output. The bubble was now a dirigible; instead of narrowing, the current account deficit reached a whopping 25 percent of the GDP in 2006.

How had the hard landing been avoided? To begin with, Iceland had become a member of the common European labor market in May 2006, effectively removing all barriers between the island and migrating workers from the Continent. Much of that labor force was supplied by Poland and the Baltic countries that had recently joined the EU; given the low wage level at home, these workers embarked on a great western migration. The Icelandic krona was strong enough to attract workers at a rate of 1,000 people per month (adjusted for population size, this influx would be comparable to a million immigrants in the United States a month).

This was no less than a paradigm shift. Historically, labor shortages had produced bottlenecks during the Icelandic economic upswings, since the unemployment rate was almost always very low, around 2 percent. Now, thousands of ready new workers swelled the labor supply by 6 to 7 percent in one year. By the end of 2006, about 9 percent of the labor force was foreign born, a 4 percent jump from 2005. Naturally, housing rents in Reykjavik had appreciated steeply.

Recent crisis be damned, the carry trade came back to town with a vengeance in the summer of 2006. The central bank acted as a welcome wagon by raising interest rates to nearly 14 percent to strengthen the ISK and contain inflation. High interest rates in a small, open economy not only attract foreign capital but provide the domestic market with the incentive to borrow in foreign currency. Sure enough, speculators inside and out took the bait. First, hedge fund carry traders were lured in. Then issuing of glacier bonds resumed with furor. Meanwhile, the pumped-up ISK boosted purchasing power for Icelandic households and underwrote a spending boom.

The last piece of the puzzle was political in nature. National elections were scheduled for the spring of 2007; the gigantic fiscal boost was a direct play to win over votes. The Icelandic government had taken heat at home and abroad for its lax fiscal policy, and the election year budget just showed that the political leadership had taken no heed of these warnings. Since revenues in Iceland are derived mostly from indirect taxation—such as a 24.5 percent value added tax on most consumer items—a spending boom always produces benefits for national coffers. Thus, the government maintained a surplus throughout the boom despite steady spending increases. It can even be argued that its budgeting was neutral rather than expansive. Either way, two governing parties were intent on delivering the mother of all election budgets, a weighty mix of pork barrel spending and deep tax cuts. Its immediate effect was a 5 percent increase in households' purchasing power in the first quarter of 2007.

The macroeconomic development of Iceland from 2006 to 2008 demonstrates that independent monetary policy in an interconnected world of free factor flows is futile, while the consequences of misguided policy are profound. Nevertheless, Iceland's boiling economy was not the engine that drove the stock market boom; rather, higher stock prices created wealth effects, which in turn drove the real economy. Iceland's housing bubble and lending boom were massive, evidenced by the proliferation of construction sites swarmed over by Slavic-speaking workers, but not atypical. In fact, its bubble was more benign than in other European countries, since it had less time to inflate.

The country had been more or less exempt from the global housing boom of the 1990s, due to the state's strict controls on mortgage lending and the banks' role as lenders being a secondary one. Housing prices first spiked when the banks moved into the market in 2004, but just two years later all three of Iceland's banks had applied the brakes to their lending in this sector; by 2007, the average loan-to-value ratio in their mortgage portfolios was between 50 and 60 percent. Research conducted by the central bank in March 2009 shows that 89 percent of households held their mortgage debt solely in domestic currency, 3 percent in foreign currency, and 8 percent in a mix—ample proof that the banks were reluctant to use anything besides the krona in mortgages. These lending practices qualify as conservative both in terms of leverage and foreign currency exposure, especially when compared with the practices of the United States, Eastern Europe, Spain, or Ireland.

Population pressure and rising incomes had a greater effect on the Icelandic housing market than any other factors. Households were indeed leveraged but not grossly so, given the ownership rate of 80 percent and demographics weighted toward the young. Even after an 80 percent depreciation of the krona and a 25 percent decline in the real prices of houses by the end of 2008, about 80 percent of households retained positive equity in their homes. Iceland mirrored many Western nations in the excessive lending on the value of inflated asset prices, but, unlike most of those countries, its housing sector did not inflate the bubble.

⇥ LIVING IN A BUBBLE ⇤

The Icelandic bubble is best explained by stock market exuberance. Given the prominent role played by investment banking and holding companies, the most apt comparison is with the Roaring Twenties in America that led up to the stock market crash of 1929. Since Icelandic investors really were not betting on their own economy, most observers were not overly concerned by the prospect that history might repeat itself, with the boom ending in a hard landing. So the investors continued to place bets on the world equity markets, but on a scale likely unprecedented in the world's financial history.

Companies operating on a small, distant island do not have the luxury of a piecemeal approach to their expansion. Once they hit the limits of their domestic markets, they must either take a giant leap overseas or be content with stasis at home. A savvy business plan is not preparation enough. Aspiring multinationals also must have access to equity and debt financing to break through in larger markets. Little wonder, then, that the financial sector called these cross-border expansions *útrás*, literally translated into English as "outward attack." This term, along with many other images, symbols, and phrases employed during the expansion, was borrowed from the Sagas: words attributed to Old Norse chieftains became common in the public discourse.

Throughout the centuries, Iceland had come to feel like a fortress, which provided comfort at the price of isolation. By the end of the twentieth century, its people were tired of waiting for multinationals to make the first move toward an integration with world markets. When Kaupthing challenged the government's monopoly on mortgages in 2004, Sigurdsson proclaimed on national television that "we are the international-foreign bank people have been waiting for." The banks had broken out of their own fortress walls by securing foreign loan financing. With little equity at the outset, they took care with their initial acquisitions to ensure that they received good value. They lucked into good timing, and benefited by shunning the dot-com bubble; after 9/11, equity came cheap for them.

From 2003 to 2005, shareholders in these *útrás* received rich rewards that the banks could not fail to notice. Kaupthing, then Landsbanki, and last Glitnir, at the tail end of the boom, all waged their own *útrás*. By 2006, all three had constructed international banking platforms, while their actions were mimicked by smaller players in the domestic market. The revenue models needed fees, large concentrations of equity called for returns, and employees were hungry for bonuses and returns on their stock options. But here, again, the country's diminutive population created a shallow pool of potential employees. The limited domestic opportunities led to a cross-border, leveraged buyout frenzy, which could be viewed as a good concept taken to unfortunate extreme, industriousness shifting into hyperactivity.

Útrás became a cultural phenomenon, and every second business, it seemed, was trying to leap outside the country. The business schools theorized about what made Icelandic entrepreneurship "special"; considering the profile of champions like Jón Ásgeir Jóhannesson, perhaps it is unsurprising that the special ingredients were identified as fast decision-making, informal workplaces, tireless work ethic, and can-do spirit. *Útrás* ran their successful course, after which the banks relaxed their lending rules and foreign acquisitions were carried out with much less concern for value.

By 2006 the *útrás* was past its prime as a viable growth strategy as it had become a "me too" journey of all kinds of business that used the all too available loan financing from the banks to purchase companies abroad. At the same time the banks themselves became the focal points of the *útrás*. In February 2005, Prime Minister Halldór Ásgrímsson publicly floated the idea of making the nation into a new global financial center. To achieve this, Ásgrímsson maintained, "we have to have our goals clear and keep on going on the same road and show the same daring that we have shown so far." The response received nearly unanimous popular support.

And why not? The banks were wonderful milking cows, paying high taxes and creating good jobs and wealth that was trickling into almost every corner of the country. It was difficult in such a heady time to see the downside to the strategy. The national institutions had no resources that would enable them to serve as a lender of last resort for the banks or to offer guarantees to their creditors. What was more, the unhealthy competition among the giants led to an inevitable relaxation of the lending standards. These facts did not seem prohibitive or alarming in the good times. With every year the boom lasted, the number of skeptics would diminish, until at the very end there were almost none, even as the fundamentals of the fabled *útrás* were getting weaker and weaker. The five-year boom also had a decadent effect on the stock market, making investors too complacent and insensitive to risk. In that respect the story of the Icelandic financial markets parallels that of the world.

The Icelandic bankers were not villains or fools, however tempting those labels may be in hindsight. They were aggressive investors and lenders, and their biggest fault was a willingness to accept equity as collateral. Iceland had funneled much of its top human capital into them. Indeed, the Icelanders often displayed more cunning in their operations than other investment banks—U.S. banks, for instance— by mostly steering clear of the subprime credit derivative bubble. They were wholesale funded, but after the Geyser crisis they managed their funding far more sensibly, with a longer maturity profile, than most of their foreign competitors. But they worked in unique circumstances, in a financial system centered on foreign-funded investment banks with an incredibly high level of systemic risk. The biggest difference between the Icelandic banks and the banks abroad was first and foremost the level of assistance their government would be able to grant in times of crisis.

It is also important to remember that despite being an early casualty of the global crisis, Icelanders were not alone in their bullishness. Most financial institutions, especially investment banks, were delivering extravagant returns in 2005–2007 and their stock was favored by analysts. The established financial centers, such as London, all contributed to the unsustainable boom times and will in all likelihood take a hard hit due to the crisis. Speculation on consolidation and cross-border integration was all the rage in European banking; it was assumed that many European financial companies eventually should trade at some "takeover" premium. This was especially true of Scandinavia, which was home to many small and midsize banks that seemed ripe for either merger or acquisition. The new center-right government in Sweden was contemplating the sale of its shares in Nordea, which many believed would be a starting point in a Scandinavian consolidation. But the fierce 2007 fight between Barclays and Royal Bank of Scotland to acquire the Dutch bank ABN Amro better defines the spirit of the immodest era. RBS won the bid and bought the bank for $98.3 billion that October; the telling coda is that RBS is now all but nationalized.

The first years of the century had shown great promise. But it was not until late 2006—following a crisis that had looked like the end—that funding constraints truly seemed unlimited, thanks to structured U.S. credit. It is now breathtaking to consider just how much foreign leverage the Icelanders amassed in less than two years. This is evidence enough of the worldwide credit bubble. During Geyser, Iceland was criticized harshly for hosting a banking system five times the size of its economy, with an external debt three times the GDP, but two years later, those figures, unbelievably, had nearly doubled.

Of course there were assets against these debts and many of them were held abroad. Asset bubbles in small, open economies are invariably inflated by foreign leverage that is then used to buy domestic assets; this then creates a currency mismatch between the assets and liabilities. Meanwhile, the banks play the carry trade and take out loans at cheap foreign rates—in yen and Swiss francs, for instance—then relend at the higher domestic rate.

Here again, Iceland's bubble had its own way of doing things. Its bankers used foreign leverage mainly to buy assets abroad or at least in Icelandic companies that had their own foreign operations. They also were immersed in a reverse carry trade to offload currency risk, which will be explained in more detail in the next chapter. Last, their bets were mostly on foreign markets. An odd arrangement indeed, but for a long time it worked beautifully. The foreign net asset position of the country improved throughout the golden decade of 1997 to 2007. For the first time, Iceland had a class so wealthy that many of its members made it to *Forbes*'s list of the richest global citizens, and it didn't take long for their spending to trickle through a population of 300,000.

But these individuals and their companies had bet the farm on one supposition about their equity premium, namely, that their stock would always outperform bonds over time. They also underestimated the liquidity premium of holding equity, that is, the precarious access to the international markets that funded their positions. And they did not consider that in a liquidity crisis, the fundamentals of a stock are of little consequence. So it was that most of the equity wealth accumulated in Iceland evaporated in the liquidity crisis that began in August 2007.

A tragic finale, then, was in store for those who enjoyed the bubble of 2005–2007, or was it comic? After the stock of cod collapsed in 1988, the Icelanders seemed to do everything right. They had privatized and liberalized, they had opened their arms to the world at large, and when no one answered they went forth to seize the fruits of globalization with both hands. Their self-reliance and self-assuredness served them well throughout. Had they heeded the warnings and called it quits after the Geyser crisis, they could have divested their foreign equity investment at a huge profit, as is true of all speculators. But of course, being spoiled as gamblers, they were unable to quit while ahead. With each goal attained, new and more challenging ones were set at once. Overbearing ambition took down the best.

It is sometimes said that the life of each person will be judged by its end. If that is so, it would be sad indeed if the great accomplishments of over 20 years of creative hyperactivity were to be judged by the total collapse of the Icelandic financial system in 2008.

CHAPTER 6

THE ROAD TO PERDITION

THE PLOT AT THE 101 HOTEL

On Thursday night, January 31, 2008, a group of Kaupthing traders and analysts arrived at the bar of 101, one of Reykjavik's trendiest hotels. They had been invited by an exceptionally buoyant group of foreign investors, who turned out to be a pack of hedge fund managers collected together by dealers and investors from Merrill Lynch and Bear Stearns.

The group had just arrived in the country, but clearly they had availed themselves to plenty of free drinks in the business class section of their inbound flight. The leader, from the Icelanders' perspective, seemed to be "Joe," a white-haired American in his mid-fifties, with a floral complexion. He looked more like a New York City cop than a buccaneer and was amusing to watch, less so to listen to.

Joe was restless. He bounced among the guests and quickly took one aside to burble a curious warning. "Boy, you are in tight spot. These people"—he pointed to his drinking companions— "are your enemies.

All the people in this party are shorting Iceland, except me. They think Iceland will be the place for the second coming of Christ, a new financial Armageddon." Joe's speech seemed to be in fast-forward mode, his message too urgent to contain. "You need to call a friend," he said. "Can you tell me how you plan to possibly save yourself from the situation so that I can convince them to stop shorting you?"

The "party" moved on to the Seafood Cellar, one of the town's most celebrated restaurants. Still, Joe could not sit still, nor did he seem to need to eat. Just after 10 p.m.—two hours into the revelry—he simply disappeared. His compatriots, however, were just getting started, although by this point one had passed out. The wine kept flowing and the hedge fund managers, their tongues loosening, confirmed Joe's warning by loudly boasting of their short positions. The Icelanders grew ever more uneasy as the conversation shifted into interrogation and mockery. It was soon apparent that their hosts were a contemptuous lot who were convinced they had landed in a country full of rubes.

The Kaupthing reps managed to leave without a fight breaking out, and they were glad to escape, like their "friend" Joe, into the cold winter night. But they were also well aware that for a hedge fund, taking down a nation through financial positioning is not just a commendable goal but an ego booster.

A month after this curious event, on February 29, a Bear Stearns analyst who had been part of the group published a report on the Icelandic trip. "Kazakhstan: A Comparison with Iceland" stated that "we have visited both Iceland and Kazakhstan, two countries which recently have been in the market's eye because of concern for overheating economies on the back of arguably overly aggressive expansion of their banking systems." Further, it recommended opposite positions with respect to the two countries: long on Kazakhstan, short on Iceland.

The report's overview reads like a bizarre exercise in macroeconomics; beyond the facts quoted above, it is extremely difficult to find anything that these countries have in common. Nevertheless, one keen observation stung Icelandic pride to the quick. The country had external liabilities roughly five times the GDP and official foreign reserves of about $2.6 billion, or 15 percent of the GDP. By contrast, Kazakhstan had external liabilities of about 100 percent of GDP but official reserves of about 40 percent. In other words, it did not matter how developed, sophisticated, or rich anyone was if they were not liquid in a time of crisis. As risible as Bear Stearns's macroeconomic analysis was, this point would stick. The world was in financial crisis by this time, and Iceland indeed was becoming short of liquidity.

And despite the buffoonery, "friend" Joe had been right to point out that Iceland was in big trouble by early 2008. The global crisis intensified in December and the ICEX felt the squeeze. On January 9, Gnúpur, an investment company, was one of the first to throw in the towel and be liquidated by the banks. Gnúpur was small fry, but nevertheless this news prompted concern abroad. Glitnir, which saw a U.S. fund-raising show upstaged by Gnúpur's collapse, aborted a planned new bond issue. Kaupthing's operations were also disrupted. In August 2007, just when the crisis arose, it had announced an acquisition—of NIBC, a Dutch bank—that would almost double its balance sheet. The deal required a new share issue in the first quarter of 2008, but in the wake of bad news the markets questioned the viability of the deal and the ability of Exista, Kaupthing's largest shareholder, to buy the newly issued shares.

It was therefore no surprise when on January 11, a Morgan Stanley's fixed income research report (titled "Iceland—Unsustainable") cited these events while arguing for a short position against the Icelandic banks. Kaupthing's credibility was further compromised when it called off the NIBC acquisition on January 30 (the day before Joe came to town), under pressure from the Icelandic Financial Supervision Agency (FSA). Simultaneously, the credit crisis in the United States had direct effect on the banks, as more and more CDOs containing subprime mortgages went into default and their content was put on the market at fire sale prices. Many of these CDOs also contained Icelandic banking bonds, or long CDS positions on those bonds; thus, the credit market suddenly was flooded with Icelandic debt. The CDS spread, which had been about 50 basis points above the Libor in August, reached 200 points by year's end. This metric helped distinguish Iceland as the weak deer in the herd, which brought the hedge funds in for the kill in 2008. When Joe and his companions arrived, the CDS spread on the banks stood between 200 and 400; a month later, when Bear Stearns's Iceland-Kazakhstan comparison appeared, it had widened to 700.

Furthermore, on January 28, Moody's published a "special comment" titled *Iceland's AAA Ratings at a Crossroads*. Inside, a stark question was posed: "How can such a highly leveraged economy be rated AAA?" Moody's repeatedly had defended this rating in the past, facilitating the flow of billions of dollars into the country; but the comment noted "conditions in the global credit markets have changed radically," and concluded that "Moody's top rating must be applied only to those countries able to manage a changing reality." The writing was on the wall. Just two days later, on January 30 , (the day before Joe and friends came to town) Moody´s downgraded Glitnir and Landsbanki on "concerns with regard to the Icelandic banks' market-sensitive business model." Kaupthing, left on negative watch for the time being, was downgraded to A1 on February 28; Glitnir and Landsbanki took a second downgrade to A2 the same day. The age of downgrades had dawned in Iceland, and although the ratings were still way above what the CDS spreads implied, the signal was clear: the international financial community was deserting the island.

Joe and company were likely shorting the Icelandic banks—and the Icelandic republic—through the CDS market. While his fund had about $1 billion to $2 billion under management, neither he nor any of the 101 plotters were central to the action. Their boozy hubris had been just that; in fact, they were late arrivals to a game that had attracted far bigger, more sophisticated players.

It is likely that many hedge funds were shorting Iceland at this time, but the leaders of the pack were old "friends." These were London entities that had shorted the country in the Geyser crisis of 2006

and kept a close eye on the island afterward; they retained prominent Scandinavian employees, typically Norwegians, who knew Iceland well. Some were executing a double play by simultaneously
shorting the banks in the CDS and equity market; others, undoubtedly, were attacking through the currency market as well.

Even after its own fate was sealed, Kaupthing could savor a thin
sliver of irony: of all the institutions represented on that wild January night in Reykjavik, theirs would be the last to go down. Bear
Stearns collapsed first, after losing most of its liquidity in three days.
An emergency Federal Reserve loan on Friday, March 14, managed
to keep the bank afloat long enough to be practically given away to
JP Morgan that weekend by federal authorities. The dissolution of
such a large player sent shock waves around the globe and affected
international markets. The rise in CDS spreads coincided with the
growing mistrust of international banking, which next manifested in
a sudden, enormous widening of the iTraxx financial index. But like
a volcano that is due to erupt, yet not quite primed for the big blast,
the crisis abated after the Bear Stearns takeover. Central banks
enacted liquidity-enhancing measures around the same time, and by
the end of March the iTraxx, which had jumped to 150, was once
again below 100.

It was a different story with the CDS spreads of the Icelandic banks,
however. These continued to widen until, on March 25, they reached
1,000 points above Libor: compare this with the "worrisome" level of
100 points the banks reached at the peak of the Geyser crisis!

On March 7, just days before the run on Bear Stearns, the Icelandic currency market collapsed; the ISK lost about 20 percent of
its value in the next two weeks. The international spotlight fixed on
the banks yet again, and as before the news reports were grim. In
response, foreign corporate clients began to withdraw their deposits.
While some still doubted that Iceland was under attack by speculators, others now wondered if the debate, coupled with the dire CDS
spread, would so shake confidence in the financial system as to make
the worst-case scenario a self-fulfilled prophecy.

On March 28, at an annual general meeting of the CBI, the governor of the central bank, David Oddsson, declared that "there is an unpleasant odor of unscrupulous dealers who have decided to make a last stab at breaking down the Icelandic financial system." He called for an international investigation into attempts to drive Iceland's economy "to its knees."

"They will not get away with it," he said. Nevertheless, the CDS spreads kept moving higher. Then came the weekend.

Many had wondered if hedge funds were feeding damaging and even erroneous information to the UK press in order to better advance their short case against Iceland. These suspicions were confirmed when two UK Sunday papers, on March 30, published news items about Icesave, Landsbanki's Internet savings accounts, under almost identical headlines. In the Sunday *Times:* "Icesave gets the chill from the credit crisis. UK savers are pulling funds out of the Iceland's banks on fears it could be hard hit in the turmoil." And in the *Observer:* "Icelandic banks feel the chill as credit crunch stretches north."

The central fact of the stories was false: Icesave was not suffering a run. But a run could be incited, quite easily, by steamy headlines. Icelanders were convinced the story had been planted, but it took a phone call with a friendly UK journalist to confirm that a number of "helpful" hedge funds had voluntarily provided the press with information about Icelandic banks. Kaupthing lawyers had put in calls to both the *Times* and the *Observer* immediately after the stories were published, and both promptly published retractions.

Quick thinking was necessary to devise an effective counterattack and restore confidence in the financial system. It was next to impossible to implicate directly the hedge funds behind the attack, since the CDS market was totally opaque, but the Icelanders knew they had to drop names to have any chance of making the most aggressive funds back off.

Sigurdur Einarsson, Kaupthing's chairman, went public the next day, March 31, in the *Financial Times*. He implicated a handful of hedge funds as the culprits, but made his strongest play by stating that Kaupthing was poised to file a lawsuit against Bear Stearns, which could lead to subpoenaed e-mails and records not just from the failed broker, but even from hedge funds connected to it. In truth, such a lawsuit would have little chance of success; Einarsson's tactics were meant to draw attention to the matter and serve as a warning to hedge funds who believed their methods could never be made transparent.

The next day, Iceland's FSA opened a formal investigation into an alleged speculative attack by hedge funds on the national currency, banking system, and stock market. The agency was "searching whether some parties have systematically been distributing negative and false rumors about the Icelandic banks and financial system in order to profit from it." The investigation would proceed in the coming months in cooperation with financial authorities in neighboring countries but fail to produce decisive results due to lack of evidence.

This was an effective stroke indeed. On both sides of the Atlantic it tapped growing concern over market abuses and malicious rumors that were affecting, for example, Lehman Brothers and the UK's HBOS bank. *New York Times* columnist Paul Krugman addressed the matter on the same day Einarsson spoke out, under the headline "The North Atlantic Conspiracy." On April 2, Ben Bernanke, chairman of the Federal Reserve, was asked about the alleged attacks on Iceland while he testified before Congress. The next day, a news report on the activity appeared on the front page of the *Wall Street Journal.* The political risk of the attack was growing by the day.

Strengthened by the international attention, Iceland's prime minister, Geir Harrde, threatened direct intervention in the currency and stock markets. "We would like to see these people off our backs and we are considering all options available," he said in an interview. He refused to talk specifics. "A bear trap needs to be a surprise," he explained. He then referred to the successful direct intervention undertaken by Hong Kong authorities in the Asian crisis of 1998, in which speculators had also attempted systematic destabilization through shorting currency and stock market.

The Icelanders had won a short-term victory. The attack stopped, and the CDS spreads of the banks dropped to between 300 and 400 points in a few days; the ISK stabilized. The government had expressed its firm support of the banks and calm, if not long-term health, was restored. While the central bank's support was no longer in question, its ability to sustain that support certainly was. This was reflected in the CDS spreads, after a quick narrowing, still remaining high, in the 600–700 point range. It was imperative for the government to secure foreign currency reserves in order to become a credible backup for the banking system.

Many influential players assumed that foreign support was a given, and this was the primary reason the hedge funds turned back that spring. A Morgan Stanley report from April 4 was released with the heading "Icelandic Banks—the Risk to Your Short." It observed that, although Iceland had almost no reserves, the republic was virtually debt free in foreign currency. It could easily raise between $10 billion and $11 billion and still maintain a public debt-to-GDP ratio of about 65 percent—still on the lower end of the debt level spectrum for European nations. With facilities from other central banks committed, Morgan Stanley stated that "we can get relatively comfortable with Icelandic banks' liquidity for the rest of the year."

Foreign credit, then, was crucial to the prognosis, but all who assumed it was forthcoming were in error. The Central Bank of Iceland (CBI) would soon discover that three major central banks in the Western world had decided collectively not to assist Iceland.

⇥ THE SUMMER BEFORE THE DARK ⇤

Just months before, there had been little evidence that turbulence was waiting to return to Iceland. The summer of 2007 had been so heady a time for the ICEX that summer holidays were canceled on the trading floors of the banks due to the heavy volume. Earlier that year the largest nonfinancial company on the index—Actavis, a generic drug company—was taken private in a leveraged buyout that netted its Icelandic shareholders about $1.3 billion, cash, equivalent to about 8 percent of the GDP. Actavis, the flagship of the new Icelandic multinational corporations, had been built around a loophole in the international patent rights legislation but had since become one of the world's largest generic drug companies. Its buyout was leveraged by Thor Björgólfsson, owner of Landsbanki, with funding from Deutsche Bank. Shareholders had received multiple returns on their investment, and many plowed these proceeds back into the ballooning ICEX. By July, the ICEX market cap was above 3,000 billion ISK, almost three times the GDP of Iceland.

By this time, the banks' focus had shifted from acquiring new holdings to recruiting talent in foreign markets: teams of analysts and traders tasked with bulking up their investment banking divisions. Kaupthing concentrated on retooling Singer & Friedlander, its UK bank, as its investment platform. In fact, there were only a few Icelanders working in London; most of the star employees at S&F were seasoned investment bankers who had been lured by generous earning-share contracts. The strategy paid off: Kaupthing revenue was 22 percent above expectations for the first half of 2007, S&F's return on capital jumped 10 points, to 16 percent, from the year before. These numbers triggered a "Company Flash" from Citigroup equity research on July 26, which was titled "Strong Results, Management Upbeat" and included a strong buy recommendation. Kaupthing's shares were up by 44 percent from the beginning of 2007, but Citigroup believed that a 20 percent upside was still in the cards. This was the high watermark of Icelandic investment banking.

Kaupthing had not made a major acquisition in two years. It was not that management had given up on acquisitive growth, but that targets were scarce: in the bull market, banks were expensive and their multiples high. Kaupthing had backed away from several deals due to price but "finally," on August 15, it announced the NIBC acquisition, with a $3 billion price tag. The transaction would enlarge the bank's balance sheet by two-thirds.

Management thought, however, that NIBC would be a bargain. A Dutch corporate bank, it was owned by JC Flowers, the world's most active financial investor. NIBC was one of the first European banks to accept losses due to exposure to subprime mortgages; write-downs had wiped out its profit from the first half of 2007. Its price to book, 1.5, and its multiples were low when compared with those of other banks. All the subprime-related assets were to be left behind in a separate vehicle that Kaupthing would partly provide with funding. NIBC shareholders would accept 46 percent of the acquisition price in shares of Kaupthing. As a result, 25 percent of Kaupthing's revenue would derive from Benelux countries, and JC Flowers would become a strategic shareholder in the bank.

Time has revealed that this was, without a doubt, the single-greatest mistake made by Einarsson and his crew. NIBC was wholesale funded and bereft of market confidence by spring 2007. Its CDS spreads were trading at Libor 800 to 1,000 basis points. Not only was Kaupthing saddled with an enormous new funding burden, the acquisition grew the banking sector yet another size larger relative to the national GDP. Already facing heavy criticism for their reliance on wholesale funding and foreign leverage ratio, the Icelanders were brazenly assuming more.

Then came the international liquidity crisis in August, and a quick slide into darkness.

Icelanders were as surprised as most everyone else in the world's financial markets when the crisis hit. Most people believed that the subprime debt delinquency was a problem isolated in the United States. As it turned out, the uncontainable crisis spread and deepened with extraordinary speed, and it overturned all traditional, accepted norms of central and commercial banking.

But this time, Iceland played the role of the canary in a coal mine to a tee, and showed early signs of distress. The CDS spreads of its banks rose instantly, and reached 100 by September 2007.

"When clients ask us why the Icelandic banks are considered to have a higher risk profile than their other European peers," explained Richard Thomas, Merrill Lynch credit analyst in a report dated March 31, 2008, "one does not have to search hard for answers: rapid expansion, inexperienced yet aggressive management, high dependence on external funding, high gearing to equity markets, connected party opacity. In other words: too fast, too young, too much, too short, too connected, too volatile."

⇥ UNDER PRESSURE ⇤

Iceland's banks were not entirely unprepared for a new crisis. In fact, they were better off than many wholesale banks since their funding was more diversified and with a longer maturity—structuring strategies that were the fruit of having survived the Geyser crisis. Unfortunately, the events of 2006 also taught them that the best strategy in hard times was to ride out the storm. This meant, in 2007, that they were too slow in accepting that the financial world was being turned on its head; they also waited to reduce leverage and sell off assets.

As the crisis progressed, it seemed ever more difficult to deleverage except by selling assets at steep discounts that cut into their equity positions and broke covenants on existing bond issues. Breach of covenants would have led to early redemption demands on key parts of the banks' funding. This placed the banks in a catch-22. On one hand, the crisis seemed to demand that some weight be shed; on the other, the banks' expansion strategy had been fueled by a virtuous cycle of foreign acquisitions and ratings upgrades that would be reversed if they began selling their holdings abroad. What was more, all banking assets were now trading at large discounts, which meant that sales would result in booked losses and a drop in equity. This helps explain why the combined balance sheet of the banks had shrunk by only 7 percent, measured in euros, by 2008.

Landsbanki, which had very little wholesale debt maturing in 2008, was in the best position at the outset. Icesave, the Internet deposit system had been founded in the UK in October 2006, and it proved to be an important outlet indeed. Since Icesave operated without any retail branch network or any associated fixed costs, it could pay out higher rates than its British competitors and attract more depositors. By mid-2007, Landsbanki's deposit-to-loan ratio had leapt to 70 percent, more than a two-fold increase. Icesave was utilized not just by individuals but also by institutions, such as charities, municipalities, the London police, and Oxford University. Since retail deposits are considered to be a much more stable source of funding than capital markets, Icesave was applauded by rating agencies and credit analysts alike. However, there was a strange disconnect between the ratings agencies, banking analysts, and sovereign analysts. Whereas the banking analysts applauded Icesave, the sovereign analysts took no note of the increased contingent liability of the state through it's deposit guarantee.

As a result, Landsbanki's CDS spreads were 200 to 300 points lower than its two competitors throughout most of the crisis. Its stock price actually rose in October 2007 as at first glance it looked as if the bank would benefit from the liquidity crisis after UK savers pulled out of stocks and bonds and ran for cover in state-guaranteed accounts.

The hitch with retail funding is its exposure to "headline risk": negative news coverage that can affect its customers' confidence and, in the worst case, trigger a run of withdrawals. In 2008, the fear in Icelandic financial industry was that contagion between financial wires and popular media could result in a run on Landsbanki, which in turn could jeopardize the country itself; after all, the accounts were under the aegis of Icesave, and they had an Icelandic deposit guarantee. What was more, Northern Rock, a small UK retail bank, had suffered a run in September 2007, the first bank run in Europe for 70 years, which was stopped only when the bank was nationalized. This episode did not have much direct impact on Icesave, which actually saw an increase in accounts as UK investors sought to spread out their deposits. But it did influence actions of the British authorities later in 2008, when it was the Icelanders' turn to suffer a similar run on their banks.

On the second tier was Kaupthing, which was weakened by the pending acquisition of NIBC as well as a failed attempt at empire building on the part of its main owner, Exista. Exista recently had leveraged up to buy a 20 percent share in Sampo, a Finnish insurance company, and Kaupthing likewise had bought a 20 percent stake in Storebrand, a Norwegian insurance company. Being leveraged *and* saddled with a low equity ratio is a poor stance to take in the face of a liquidity crisis. Both Exista and Kaupthing were using valuable capital and liquidity to hold listed equity on their books.

Until the NIBC deal was called off, Kaupthing's CDS spreads were the highest among the three banks. The good news was that Kaupthing's load of maturing debt was relatively light—EUR 2 billion. Also, it launched its own Internet banking account firm, Kaupthing Edge, first in Finland in October 2007, shortly afterwards in Sweden and then in the UK in January. The Edge accounts concept was similar to Icesave's, with a crucial difference: Icesave was under the Icelandic deposits guarantee scheme backed up by the nation's taxpayers. The Edge operated under the auspices of the host country, from which the deposits were drawn. By the second quarter of 2008, it was having a marked effect on the bank's deposit-to-loan ratio, and by September the liquidity situation had improved dramatically as well.

Glitnir's funding profile brought up the rear, by a wide margin. It had EUR 2.4 billion debt maturing in 2008 (with a balance sheet half the size of Kaupthing's), and its attempt at Internet savings, in Norway, was too late and too limited in scope to turn things around. The bank did have good assets in Norway that could be sold off with a profit or pledged for cash.

Nevertheless, after its U.S. road show to issue new banking bonds proved a bust, it was clear that the Glitnir funding model was broken. Knowing full well that the demise of one meant the demise of all, Landsbanki and Kaupthing began to discuss in early 2008 how the bank might be acquired and its assets split between them. A merger or takeover of Glitnir by the two others would have to be assisted by the government and the CBI in some way, but no leadership was coming from the authorities and distrust and animosity among the managers of banks was not helping. As the crisis progressed, the subject was revisited many times without any action being taken.

From an outsider's perspective, there were mitigating factors that favored Iceland's banks. Foreign credit analysts perceived that they had problems with liquidity, to be sure, but not with capital. Their equity ratio going into the crisis was higher than that of their Scandinavian counterparts, for example. Most important, they held almost no credit derivatives—which were the first items of collateral damage of the crisis. Meanwhile, the economy at large hummed along nicely in the first year of the crisis. Significant increases in export revenue supplanted slowly declining consumption. As a large exporter of both food and energy, Iceland therefore stood to benefit from the skyrocketing price of both items in 2007–2008. The new Alcoa aluminum smelter on the east side of the island was set to begin production in 2008, which would further increase export revenue.

The banks continued to play the carry trade in reverse, hedging their equity with short positions against their own currency. While it may seem counterproductive to bet, in effect, against one's own team, in fact they had no other options. On average, about 70 percent of their aggregate balance sheet was denominated in foreign currency, either through operations abroad or domestic lending. With these numbers, keeping the equity in ISK meant that currency depreciation would automatically lower the equity ratio, since a lower value of currency means that the price of foreign items rises. Since Icelandic law required that the banks use the krona as the operating unit of account, converting the equity into foreign currency was the equivalent of taking a short position. Kaupthing actually had begun to hedge out part of its equity in 2005, following the acquisition of S&F, but by late 2007 all three banks were rapidly converting their equity into euros. Many large investment companies followed suit.

At the end of 2007, most Icelandic economists expected the ISK to depreciate in the coming year, with the global crisis still in effect. Nevertheless, the currency and the carry trade held up quite well at first, and the issuing of glacier bonds kept up at a remarkable pace. The CBI also maintained a 10 percent interest rate differential to support the ISK and to keep inflation at bay.

When the currency market finally tanked during the speculation attack, there was a jump in the banks' capital ratio; Kaupthing, for example, received a £1 billion equity boost in the first quarter. Since inflationary spikes always increased bank profit in Iceland, a second booster was in store via ISK depreciation. The pass through into higher prices in the domestic market is both rapid and widespread, given that about 40 percent of all personal consumption is imported. Also, inflation increases the loan margin of the banks, since most out-going loans denominated in ISK are indexed, even though the banks are legally forbidden to offer indexation on short-term deposits.

Currency depreciation and inflation typically destroy banks in small, open, and emerging economies in financial crisis. The Icelanders had created defenses against both foes, at least in the short-term, as evidenced by the profits they booked up to the moment they collapsed. In the long term, currency depreciation and inflation will visit negative effects on the client base and loan quality; indeed, the asset quality of Iceland's banks suffered more and more as the crisis deepened. Liquidity dried up and global equity markets continued to take a beating. The ICEX performed worse than any other European index; by January 2008, it had shed 40 percent of its value since the summer, and loan-to-collateral ratios were in even worse shape. The Icelanders were able to see the trouble these figures posed behind their profits. They feared they were trapped in a downward spiral, in which each margin call made on a leveraged stock position would lead to a further market sell-off, which in turn would trigger new margin calls, further sell-offs, ad infinitum. There simply were no buyers.

It was, in one sense, an enormous game of dominoes. The banks believed they could not allow any large investment company to fail for fear of toppling all the rest. What followed was a de facto dismantling of margin calls as a tool to recover loans made out on the value of equity as collateral. The banks attempted to find new homes for stocks by lending them to other investment companies but on weakening collateral.

Foreign banks, of course, continued to make margin calls. In the first month of 2008 they withdrew much of the funding that had been lent directly to the Icelandic investment companies in 2006–2007 and contributed mightily to the asset bubble. The three banks, again fearing for the safety of the system, became the lenders of last resort for these investment companies whose assets had been rendered illiquid as the foreign banks withdrew. This placed greater strain on their liquidity position, but every investment company was considered too systemically important to be liquidated by an outside margin call. Practically all of these investment companies had large stakes in one of the banks; the banks were bailing out their owners.

The hedge funds were still eager to short the stocks of the banks or, as a next-best alternative, to short-list companies abroad that had Icelanders as major shareholders and perhaps force an asset sale. Shorting an Icelandic stock was not just a bet against a particular company but a bet against the currency as well, since all stocks were denominated in ISK. But there was a catch: to short a stock (sell it forward) one must borrow it first. Since most Icelandic stocks were held domestically, shorting was not such an easy game for foreigners. However, as the liquidity crisis deepened, it became more lucrative for an Icelandic party to lend stock to hedge funds, since they could realize 30 to 40 percent in annual interest.

Kaupthing's stock was probably shorted most often since it was the most liquid, largest, and most widely held in the country, and it also had a second listing in Stockholm. The pervasiveness of the short position can be demonstrated by the bank's stock being traded at a significantly positive price on the Swedish stock exchange (2 Swedish krona per share, or 4 to 5 percent of the precollapse market value) even after it had defaulted. Hedge funds wanting to close short positions kept up demand.

The domino approach to evaluating collateral in stock lending did in fact slow the price decline in the ICEX. By late summer 2008, the banks, Kaupthing especially, were trading at high multiples as compared with their Scandinavian counterparts, and especially considering their CDS spreads. But the strategy bought little more than time. The financial system had become hopelessly entangled through cross-lending systemic risk, especially once bank funding replaced foreign direct lending. More and more the banks looked like Siamese triplets, vitally connected through lending on the value of each other's shares.

It has to be kept in mind that although the Icelandic banks were big in comparison to their home country, they were small on the international scene and not especially large when compared to many of their clients. Through their investment banking activities they had played a leading role in financing comparatively large cross-border acquisitions for the upstart multinationals, and their credit exposure was quite concentrated to begin with. Rescue lending in the early part of 2008 further exacerbated this situation; in 2008, the Icelandic banks had about 23 exposures in their loan books larger than 10 percent of their equity, between 6 to 10 in each bank. The majority of these exposures were to holding companies.

By the time the 2008 crisis peaked, almost all of these holding companies had become too big to fail in the Icelandic financial system. Important clients inevitably come to wield power over their lenders, but in one sense the exceptional nature of this crisis allowed the banks to turn the tables. They began to press big clients, like Baugur, to sell off their holdings silently, without inciting a panic abroad or awakening the hedge funds. But despite these upsets in the bank-client relationship, the banks' management could only watch as the credit quality continued to worsen as 2008 progressed.

The banks had responded to crisis by jumping clear of wholesale and into retail funding through Internet deposits. The move had a dual purpose, since it also aided recapitalization. All three banks' bonds were trading at a huge discount (25 to 40 percent, depending on the maturity); if they could obtain enough funds via the Internet to swing a buyback of their bonds, they could book the discount from par value as a pure profit. Essentially, this was an arbitrage between wholesale and retail funding that had the potential to become intensely profitable.

Landsbanki and Kaupthing were well positioned in this gambit and pursued it aggressively; Glitnir, the weak sister, still had no luck attracting retail deposits. Despite this, the system as a whole was buoyed for a time, but one man's solution is another's problem. Foreign central banks were far from assured by this switch to retail.

⊰ IN NO-MAN'S-LAND ⊱

The Icelandic banking expansion engine received a green light when the country became a member of the European Economic Area (EEA) in 1994. Becoming a member of the EEA can best be understood as acquiring backdoor access to the greater European Union. The flow of goods, labor, capital, and services among member countries was unimpeded, and those countries in turn worked EU directives and regulations into their legal frameworks. By joining, Iceland could access the common European market without becoming subject to the conditions of full EU membership.

The EEA agreement traces its roots to a club of countries outside the EU that formed a free trade alliance called EFTA. EFTA once included countries like Britain and the Scandinavian countries, as well as Switzerland. In the early part of the 1990s, there was a partial economic merger between the two unions with EEA agreement. However, shortly afterwards almost all of the EFTA countries joined the EU, leaving only Iceland, Norway, and Liechtenstein in the EFTA part of the contract. The remaining EFTA countries were allowed to tap into the economic benefits of the European Union without having to become embroiled in EU politics. To Icelanders, it was an arrangement that provided the economic gravy while keeping them clear of the European Common Resource Policy, which might have forced them to share their fishing grounds with other EU nations. As EEA members, they were also not permitted formal membership in the European Monetary Union, a requisite for countries that wished to adopt the euro, but this fact carried far less weight in 1994.

With this "European passport," Icelandic banks could now do business throughout the EU and establish or acquire subsidiaries and branches without undue administrative oversight. But it was also exposed to systemic problems. The primary flaw could be described as a lack of commonality. The EU has a common market in financial services and a common legal framework that provides regulation, but there is no common supervisor, no common deposit guarantee system, no common lender of last resort (except perhaps in the Eurozone), and no common mechanisms for solvency support in the event of major, cross-border bank failures. Oversight is guided by the Home Country Control Principle, which implies that each country's government and central bank will take charge in the event of emergency.

There is a saying, sometimes attributed to Charles Goodhart, a professor at the London School of Economics, that international banks are only international in life. In death, they are domestic. This helps define the downside to working with fewer strings attached. Financial crises must be met with systematic and political action; as an EEA member, the nation was seriously handicapped (to put it mildly) by its less-than-formal status. The EEA allowed Iceland to develop a robust international finance sector, but when big, worldwide trouble swept over the island, there was no proper international political framework to deal with it.

As stated, the Icelandic banks had made no friends in the tightly knit world of central bankers when they moved from wholesale to retail funding as the crisis deepened. They also stirred up enormous resentment among domestic banks that had to bear the fixed costs of maintaining a branch network and payment mechanism, only to be outbid by Internet upstarts. The European retail deposits market was a sleepy, cozy place after years of limited competition; now, the Icelanders were driving up the marginal costs of funding and tapping off liquidity at the worst possible time.

Many regulators were suspicious of aggressive investment banks funding themselves with government-guaranteed retail deposits. Wholesale investors are reputedly sophisticated, able to invest without state supervision. If they wanted to roll the dice by funding investment activities, it was to be at their own risk. What was more, for retail investors—private citizens—there were consumer protection issues being raised. Icesave accounts (and Kaupthing Edge accounts in three countries, among them Germany) were offered under an Icelandic deposit guarantee through a subsidiary; as these accounts grew, regulatory authorities, chiefly in the UK, grew increasingly concerned about how much protection the Icelandic authorities would be able to offer in a time of need. By September 2008, there was about £6.5 billion in Icesave accounts and wholesale deposits—about 70 percent of Iceland's GDP at the current exchange rate—a significant proportion of which was covered by the minimum Icelandic deposit guarantee and thus legally under Icelandic supervision.

By whatever means, Icelandic banks were out to draw liquidity from foreign central banks. Collateralized borrowing was another method of achieving that. This type of repo funding is, of course, commonplace; in fact it is now the second-most-important source of liquidity (after retail deposits) for commercial banks on both sides of the Atlantic. In the first year of the crisis, the time frame for the repo agreement was extended and the standards for collateral assets relaxed. This type of lending carries risk for the central banks, since they are essentially lending money to banks that use their assets as collateral. If the borrowing bank fails or if its collateral loses value, the loss is absorbed by the taxpayers supporting the central bank.

For the Icelanders, repo access to foreign central banks came through their foreign subsidiaries; they wrapped up their assets in exchange for cash. What made these exchanges controversial was that they now obtained euros by pledging *Icelandic* assets. The Central Bank of Luxembourg became the primary conduit for this action. The Iceland banks would use not just bonds with an Icelandic state guarantee but also bonds issued by *each other*, a device known in Europe as sending "love letters."

Iceland was not alone in its creativity. Rather, this was just one result of the European Central Bank's decision to relax the standards of collateralized lending. Since Iceland was an EEA member, its bonds remained eligible as collateral in the Europeans' monetary system, its conduct within the rules. Nevertheless, the ECB had reservations about both the quantity and quality of the assets the Icelandic banks were pledging. And it was certainly annoying to watch each easing of lending standards produce a fresh wave of these dubious commodities.

This unpopularity was not unexpected. The Icelanders were behaving like motherless lambs, stealing milk from other ewes and being kicked back. Their banks could not obtain liquidity backup at home, like most other commercial banks, and the ICB could not serve as a lender of last resort. Iceland's currency was the smallest in the world and the ICB was free to print as many kronur as it pleased. But even an ocean filled with kronur was of limited use to the banks, since 70 percent of their funding needs derived from foreign currency. They could attempt to convert ISK into hard currency on the Icelandic currency market, but this required a willing trading partner. For the first six months of the crisis, the banks did just that through carry trade—double-digit interest rates lured enough investors into buying ISK—but the currency market crash in March 2008 put a crimp in this method. By now, liquidity backup at home was possible only if ICB obtained foreign currency through a line (swap agreement) with another central bank, or through direct borrowing by the Icelandic state.

Not until the speculative attack following the Bear Stearns collapse did government authorities see the need to bolster the country's currency reserves. Despite the turmoil, the Icelandic republic was almost debt free in foreign currency, and rating agencies assumed that it could raise liquidity if it so chose. The plan, then, was to open lines with the neighboring central banks and shore up confidence in the Icelandic financial system abroad. Then the next step would be for the Icelandic republic to carry out a large bond issue to bolster foreign currency reserves.

The first part of this strategy failed. In April, Iceland's overtures to the U.S. Federal Reserve, the Bank of England, and the ECB were rejected. Moreover, the ECB went tough on the Icelandic banks and set strict limits on the amount of money they could obtain through collateralized lending. On the other hand, the central banks of Norway, Sweden, and Denmark each opened a EUR 500 million line to ICB in mid-May, which for a time restored some market confidence.

In early June, the Althing authorized the government to borrow up to EUR 5 billion in the international market. With JP Morgan advising, CBI organized a road show in London for a bond issue on behalf of its government. Details of the outcome have not been publicized, but media in Iceland claimed that about $2 billion to $3 billion was available to Iceland at 185 points above Libor. The offer was rejected, allegedly because the spread was high compared with the nation's rating, and accepting funds at this "high" rate was likely to diminish the nation's credibility. Then again, this rate was a little below the national CDS spread. The logic seems very flawed. CBI has, however, never shown any remorse about this fateful refusal and has always maintained that it was acting on the advice of JP Morgan. For the financial market, it brought bitter disappointment; the banks watched their CDS spreads trend upward once again.

On July 24, with the CDS spreads of the Icelandic banks again at 1000 points over Libor, Richard Thomas of Merrill Lynch published a report on the Icelandic banks called "Distress and Default." A highly critical piece, it took the Icelandic authorities to task for their inaction, which had left the market "with almost a complete information vaccuum." Richard Thomas was blunt as usual: "The market has inevitably called the bluff of the Icelandic authorities and sent CDS sky high again. It is perfectly understandable, in our view. Markets hate a vacuum and generally assume the worst when they see one." Thomas went on to ask in frustration: "Is default really the endgame here?"

"The Icelandic authorities' steps to address this have so far been inadequate in our view," he added, "and the apparent inaction has merely fanned the flames of speculation. Though there is no evidence that we are heading in this direction, it is true that default is actually a macroeconomic tool peculiarly well suited to dealing with situations of over-indebtedness."

Through the press at home, the Icelandic government vehemently denied that there was any consideration of so drastic a measure. By autumn, however, the authorities still had constructed little or no defense against another speculative attack on the nation's financial system.

More than a year later, it is still unclear why Iceland was frozen out by the three main central banks. The only public comment came from the U.S. Federal Reserve, which stated in September that *it had not understood that Iceland had needed any assistance at all.*

CBI posted an official statement concerning this issue on its Web site on October 9, 2008:

The request for assistance was well received at first in March 2008. The bank of England suggested that an analysis from the IMF on the situation would be helpful. A small IMF team went to Iceland in April which then wrote a short appraisal that in the main supported the Icelandic request, although stating very clearly that such swap agreements only bought time to address the fundamentals of the issue; that is the large size of the banks relative to the capacity of the CBI and the size of the economy. In late April the friendly attitude had turned and the three central banks rejected the plea for help. It was obvious that these foreign Central Banks were acting in collaboration.

The reason given for the central banks' inaction was that a swap agreement with Iceland would be of little or no use given the disproportionate size of the Icelandic banking system, and that the size of any agreement that might be effective would be unacceptable to the central banks. The CBI made the counterargument that the size of the line would not really matter—just obtaining a line regardless of its size would boost confidence in the Icelandic financial system and give the CBI room to deal with the situation. But to no avail.

Even today it is rumored that CBI or another government ministry bungled the application for swap facilities, either by withholding information or by pretending that everything was fine. If this is true, it means that the Icelandic authorities asked for money without ever admitting that it really was needed. Information available is insufficient to substantiate these rumors.

A logical reading of the three central banks' decision to leave Iceland without a line is straightforward. First, the cost of solving the problem might have been large, the loans necessary to buoy the country risky. Second, the Icelanders had not hatched a credible plan for deleveraging the country or cutting the banking system down to a manageable size. Third, they seemed not at all ready to abandon their international banking system, an impossible dream made real. Perhaps the central banks considered Iceland's banking sector too big—and too far gone—to rescue; perhaps they believed a hands-off approach would save the island from itself by not allowing it to borrow more money and prop up a behemoth that was doomed in any event.

Furthermore, bailing out Iceland would be a small boon to the greater good. As a small, idiosyncratic entity of international finance, Iceland could fail without threat of systemic risk for the international financial community. Although it was a Nordic country, other Scandinavians kept a safe distance from it. Most of the major Scandinavian financial institutions owned by the Icelanders, such as FIH, were fire-walled, separate entities. From the international perspective, Iceland as a country simply was *not* too big to fail.

Or was it? Iceland's banks had wide exposure to banks in the Eurozone, in excess of $30 billion, more than two-thirds of it concentrated in German banks. One would surmise that that fact at least was considered by the ECB, or by the German government at any rate. But since the analysis of Iceland's requests is still classified, it is impossible to know what facts the central banks considered.

However valid this conjecture is, it still does not go far enough. It doesn't explain why the big three withheld even token assistance that might have helped Iceland maintain confidence, much less why they turned a deaf ear when the country cried for help in the wake of the Lehman Brothers collapse. No explanation will do, unless one considers how the central banks *benefited* from Iceland's annihilation.

Staying on the sidelines meant that the central bankers could rid themselves of a nuisance. Once liquidity dried up at home, Iceland's international investment banks were out to tap it off of their neighbors' systems; they had become negative externalities for other nations. What was more, the success of their Internet banking models carried the threat of their turning into important European retail banks, even though they remained aggressively focused on investment banking. Any coordinated international efforts to enhance global liquidity with looser rules for liquidity provisions would likely benefit them, since they would get greater leverage to peddle Icelandic assets for euros.

Rumor had it that the Bank of England and the ECB had decided to open lines to Iceland at first, but changed course after heavy lobbying by their own domestic banks, which were infuriated by the online deposit gathering. Considering the furious reaction to one line opened by a central bank—in Sweden, a country where Kaupthing did brisk Internet deposit trade—the rumor is hardly implausible.

Furthermore, it is likely that Iceland was supposed to serve as a warning to other indebted small countries that they could not expect a bailout from the big central banks—they just had to face the painful task of deleveraging head on.

Iceland after all remained an anomaly, one foreigners never warmed to. There had been a standing offer to join the EU, but Icelanders themselves had never seen a need for such intimate connection, especially when the common market was so accessible. That their special friendship with the United States, forged during the cold war, had ceased to exist was a reality that eluded the political leadership until the very end. That alliance had been based on military strategy and Iceland, as an outpost from which to monitor and defend against Soviet nuclear submarines and airforce, had received assistance when it was needed. When the United States withdrew and closed its base in Keflavik in 2006, it was the end of an era.

At the end of March 2009, Kaarlo Jännäri, retired director general of the Finnish Financial Supervision Authority, produced a report on banking regulation and supervision in Iceland. It succinctly explains how the country was left out in the cold: "After all, Iceland is a very small country in the far reaches of the cold North Atlantic, and has few friends in high places outside the Nordic countries."

⇥ THE ICELANDIC POLITICAL LEADERSHIP ⇤

In the boom times, policy authorities had looked upon the banking expansion, with its bountiful tax revenue, good jobs, and infusions of national pride, as a gift with no downside. Their cheerful unpreparedness betrayed naïveté and provincialism that proved to be devastating. The government simply never allocated the resources—such as foreign reserves—needed to build an infrastructure around the three ever-growing giants.

The Icelandic FSA operational capacity had not followed the banks in their expansion and also faced severe difficulties in hiring competent staff. In 2006 there were only 45 people working for the agency that was responsible for supervising all the actors in the Icelandic financial markets, and that year the staff turnover was about

25 percent, as good employees were attracted to the financial sector. The situation had improved with a new managing director and a larger budget; in 2008 the agency had about 60 people employed and much better operational competence. Nevertheless, in hindsight it is clear that the FSA was too weak. Yet even if they had exercised keener foresight, it is doubtful the national regulatory authorities could have contained the Icelandic banking industry. The construction of the EEA leveled its members' playing field and limited their discretionary powers. After the turn of the century, Icelandic regulators had a much smaller stick in hand than did, for example, U.S. regulators, even if they had been inclined to swing it.

Moreover, expansionist fever had spread to the governing agencies. In 2005, the prime ministry appointed a committee to draft policy proposals with the objective of turning Iceland into a new international finance center. Sigurdur Einarsson was appointed chairman, and he was surrounded by a collection of high-level government officials and business leaders. However, this body's report, published in October 2006, was essentially hot air. Its proposals skipped past any meaningful actions that have any bearing on achieving the stated goal because they were either prohibitively expensive or laden with political dynamite, such as taking full membership in the EU and the euro area.

When Landsbanki began to offer the Icelandic deposit guarantee abroad, the potential hazard for taxpayers—and the country itself—was never grasped by trade publications, the political leadership or the general public. When Landsbanki's CEO, Sigurjón Árnason, described the Icesave method as "clear genius" in an interview, it was not challenged. An editorial in the January 27, 2007, edition of *Morgunbladid*, a leading Icelandic daily, declared that "the root of this great success in attracting deposits must be an interesting subject of study for marketing specialists." The business section of *Frettabladid*, another daily chose Icesave as the best business concept of 2007 (it also lavished Jón Ásgeir Jóhannesson with the title of Businessman of the Year).

Critics have pointed to the irony that Morgunbladid was owned by Björgólfur, Landsbanki's main owner, and Frettabladid by Jón Ásgeir Jóhannesson, Baugur's main owner, himself.

So when the Icelandic banks reached the edge of the cliff in 2008 in an international crisis, Iceland was saddled with a bureaucracy of domestic scope, size, and efficiency. Its regulators and central bankers enforced the common European rules concerning capital adequacy ratios and liquidity in a diligent, almost robotic manner. The country had no officials with the oversight and mandate to make independent observations about systemic risk and viability. This lack was the result, in part, of supervisory powers being spread among three or four ministries and several institutions; this muddied the division of labor, causing all channels of communication to become clogged and confused, and making coordination among the various agencies all but impossible.

A generation gap was another root cause of the paralysis. The banking and business communities were dominated by a youthful, under-40 crowd that knew little of what had occurred before the recent age of loosening regulation and openness. These leaders were bold and well-educated, but also overconfident and inexperienced. Dialogue did not come easily between them and the political bureaucracy, which was controlled by people 15 or 20 years older with no international perspective. The politicians seemed unable to fathom what was really happening, and the bankers were not inclined or able to enlighten them.

Like other Scandinavian nations, Iceland has a four-party system and a coalition government. Unlike its Nordic neighbors, however, Icelandic politics in modern times has been dominated by the center-right Independence Party, with about 30 to 40 percent of the general vote, rather than the center-left Social Democrats. Given its egalitarian antecedents, it is not surprising that Iceland never developed a taste for class-based politics; the Independence Party marched through the twentieth century under the slogan "Class with class." This was a party that collected a variety of groups and views beneath its umbrella, and its fortunes were brightest when a charismatic, unifying leader gave the rallying call. After spending the 1970s and 1980s in the wilderness without an initiative, the party returned to power in 1991 when its new leader—David Oddsson— was elected prime minister.

Like him or not—and many didn't—Oddsson (born 1948) was a natural leader. He was the son of a single mother and raised by his grandparents in a small town, one hour's drive from Reykjavik. A comedian in his youth, he could use his wit gently in politics (he liked to relate folksy wisdom inherited from his grandmother), or to sting his enemies with one-line jabs laced with sarcasm. His gifts of persuasion were remarkable; whether he was addressing private meetings, large public gatherings, or the entire nation on TV, he could move even the most stubborn and negative audience to cheer once he had spoken. This colorful exterior was tempered, not surprisingly, by his skill as a political fighter. Opponents criticized him for intransigence and intolerance of their views, and felt he would justify any means to carry out his agenda. National polling would often see him chosen as both the most and least popular politician in Iceland.

Oddsson became a mayor in Reykjavik in 1982, then an MP, before attaining the prime ministership at the age of 43. He embraced Thatcherian free-market liberalism and provided the political muscle needed to effect privatization, tax cuts, and a free market. When these measures began to bear fruit from 1995 onward, Oddsson won nationwide admiration and the Independence Party started to define itself as the guardian of prosperity. As such, it remained in power for 17 years; Oddsson held the prime minister's chair until he stepped down in 2004, at that time the longest-serving leader in Europe.

After a brief stint as a foreign minister, Oddsson became a governor of the Central Bank of Iceland in September 2005, even though he had no formal training in economics or finance, or any working experience at a financial institution. For Iceland, this was not an outrageous move, since it was commonplace to appoint former politicians to CBI irrespective of their background. What was questioned was Oddsson's having moved into his governor's chair with enough political baggage to make building mutual trust among the three banks all but impossible.

As probusiness as Oddsson's policies of the 1990s were, he took a dim view of the youthful nouveaux riches as they flexed their foreign-leveraged muscles in the face of the traditional business community. He went on record with his criticisms early. In a public speech delivered in 1999 he compared the upstarts to Russian oligarchs. It later became abundantly clear that, like Putin, Oddsson feared state capture from the rising multinationals, which he considered too big for the country. After the turn of the century, he used his office to wage what seemed to be a personal campaign against the influence of the multinationals. Baugur and its main owner, Jón Ásgeir Jóhannesson, were singled out for abuse; Oddsson referred to Jóhannesson as a "street hooligan," and worked to obstruct the younger man's acquisitive tendencies.

He also soured on Sigurdur Einarsson and Kaupthing, and sought to foil the bank's attempted purchase of stakes in the state-owned banks. The maneuvering became almost comic in 2003, when Oddsson withdrew his deposits from Kaupthing and then made a public announcement condemning Einarsson and his crew for greed and generous option contracts. Here was a national prime minister effectively trying to incite a bank run!

Despite the absurdity (or danger) of this political theater, many of Oddsson's worries were legitimate. His supporters now point to the collapse as proof that the oligarchs were taking the country to the dogs all the while. But at the time, his adversaries accused him of carrying on either a personal vendetta or a power play that undercut the country's policy of economic liberalization.

Oddsson fueled these assessments when it seemed that he had been playing favorites. As prime minister he approved the sale of 46 percent of Landsbanki to Samson Holding, with about 70 percent leverage, even though there were two higher bids on the table. Afterward, Oddsson's closest Independence Party associate, managing director Kjartan Gunnarsson, became vice chairman of the board at the new private bank. The Icelandic FSA, which opposed this sale initially, grudgingly gave approval after months of lobbying.

Jännäri's analysis of Landsbanki's privatization concludes that the deal set a legal precedent that actually accelerated the concentration of ownership in the banking sector. Baugur's takeover of Glitnir, in 2006, was impossible to reject as a result. Others have argued that Oddsson's aggression, not at all out of keeping with the Viking Sagas, actually stirred up sympathy and popular support for the oligarchs he targeted. In fact, the publicized persecutions have undoubtedly made it much more difficult for the regulatory agencies in charge to wield their power against the nouveaux riches, since they would always cry foul. Jóhannesson would, for example, frequently, and even shamelessly, play the "Oddsson card" and claim he was a victim of a political vendetta to stir up public sympathy.

By the time Oddsson moved to CBI his biases toward each bank were widely considered to be evident. Two of the banks, Kaupthing and Glitnir, were owned or controlled by "bad" oligarchs Oddsson had tried to drive out of business. Landsbanki was in the hands of "good" oligarchs, who owed much of their good fortune to him. Trust between these players was compromised by their relations with Oddsson, and consensus became unattainable. When Glitnir's funding model crumbled after its failed fundraiser in January 2008, there was an excellent case for taking action. But what action could Oddsson initiate that would not look like another eruption of a personal grudge? Such was the dilemma of an old political fighter turned central banker.*

During the early part of his career, Oddsson played an important role in opening up the country, but when internationalization had gathered steam he seems to have veered toward the isolationist camp. He was a staunch opponent of Iceland joining the European Union and would publicly attack those who would advocate that the euro supplant the ISK as the legal currency. Regarding this issue, the Independence party was almost evenly divided. The probusiness lobby of the party was generally in favor of the EU. Oddsson's faction of the party would earn the nickname "Home Rule party," a name referring back to a forerunner of the Independence party that had been very active in the struggle for independence from the Danes in the early twentieth century.

During his years as a CBI governor Oddsson seems to have come to the conclusion that the systemic press toward internationalization was threatening the viability of Iceland's sovereign institutions, the Icelandic krona not the least. He believed that the banks' expansion abroad had rendered the CBI monetary policy almost powerless, while their shameless lobbying for euro-ization and even EU membership further undermined the currency and CBI authority. After the currency market tanked in March 2008, he placed the blame squarely on the banks and attacked them openly in the media for shorting the krona. He even asked the FSA to look into the matter, but its investigation found no evidence of misconduct.

---

*Einarsson is the only bank manager who has been candid about his relationship with Oddsson since the collapse. In March 2009, he published a newspaper article in which he cataloged Oddsson's alleged mistakes and biases as governor. In the article, Einarsson accused Oddsson of leaking details from private meetings to the press; one instance concerned Kaupthing's financing proposal to take over NIBC in the summer of 2007.

Oddsson's tenure at CBI included three years leading up to the 2008 collapse. In that time, he met with Einarsson four times in official meetings. One unofficial meeting was perhaps the most memorable. The two men sat at the same table at a CBI banquet in 2007 and, during an ensuing argument, Oddsson threatened to take down Kaupthing unless it backed away from its intention to adopt the euro as an operating currency.

Meanwhile, the banks insisted that the shorting was done with the license and supervision of the CBI, and for a sound purpose: to hedge their equity ratio, given that their operational currency was ISK but 70 percent of their assets were denominated in foreign currency. Moreover, in 2006 and 2007, Kaupthing had lobbied for approval to shift its operating currency over to euros, a natural move given the scale of its international operations. But the CBI had opposed this idea vehemently, although it never clearly explained its reasoning. It seems that the central bank believed that one defection from the ISK would lead to the exodus of the entire corporate sector. Whatever the reasoning, Kaupthing and the other banks were stuck with ISK and no recourse beyond hedging their equity ratio through a reverse·carry trade.

Kaupthing had also considered moving its headquarters to another country such as Sweden or Britain. That would have implied higher corporate taxes, since Iceland's tax rate was lower than its neighbors, but simultaneously the leverage ratio of Iceland would have been slimmed down considerably. This move was first contemplated seriously after the financial crisis hit in August 2007, too late to gain traction or be fully useful. If the acquisition of NIBC had been finalized, it probably would have been a reverse takeover, and the HQ would have been transferred to Holland. Just before the collapse Kaupthing had made arrangements, due to be announced in October, to transfer all its operations outside of Iceland and into its subsidiaries Singer & Friedlander in the UK or FIH in Denmark. If implemented, the move would have downsized the mother company in Iceland considerably and relieved CBI of at least some pressure.

Oddsson's successor, both as prime minister and the chairman of the Independence Party, was Geir Haarde (born 1951). Previously finance minister and Independence vicechair, he was Oddsson's opposite in almost every way. While Oddsson was defiant, opinionated, and a brash straight talker, Haarde was polite, congenial, indecisive, and dissembling in public. One story, appearing in the yellow press, had Oddsson being asked about his successor's leadership qualities, to which he quipped, "How can you take a house-trained cat and make it into a lion?"

Others claimed that Haarde's favorite policy was to just wait and see if things improved on their own. But he was a distinguished economist (he had a master's degree from the University of Minnesota) and in time became popular. Whereas Oddsson polarized, Haarde was a unifier.

During their reign the Independents worked with three other parties in coalition governments, but they retained control of the prime ministry, the ministry of finance, and the CBI. Almost two decades of prosperity and growth had sown blissful ignorance among the top brass, who never tried to foster a policy of economic stabilization in the boom years. Oddsson had mocked economists as "econ-technicians" when they criticized the loose fiscal policy during the dot-com bubble. Once ensconced in CBI, he criticized his former colleagues for the expansionary fiscal policies they had presided over. At last he came into alignment with professional economists inside and outside the country. Much was made of the government's having raked in exorbitant tax revenue during boom years—and spent it almost instantly.

In the months after the collapse, Haarde seemed eerily disconnected from the events. In an interview with the Associated Press on November 29 he stated, "I do not feel personally responsible.... I cannot take responsibility for the actions of the banks." One has to wonder if Geir Haarde forgot to read the liability clause of his contract before becoming prime minister of the nation. True, he was not an investment banker, the republic had not accumulated foreign debt on his watch, and of course the banks were to blame for their own defaults. But a prime minister need not be Harry "The Buck Stops Here" Truman to be personally and politically responsible for seeking a solution to a financial crisis.

Jännäri's assessment does not name names:

When the culmination of the crisis was approaching, the FME [the Icelandic Financial Supervisory Authority] and the CBI expressed grave concerns and requested information from the ministries on what kind of commitments and actions the government was prepared to take. I had the impression that the sense of urgency was felt less keenly by some of the ministries' representatives than by the FME and the CBI. On the other hand, the ministries' representatives sometimes felt that they were not receiving enough information about the seriousness of the situation and therefore believed there would be time to prepare for action later.

But whoever was responsible, when the clock struck midnight no preparations had been made.

⇥ COULD ICELANDIC BANKING HAVE BEEN SAVED? ⇤

This question will also be academic until we have achieved sufficient distance from the events of 2007–2008, and beyond. What is certain is that with larger foreign reserves and lines to major central banks, Iceland easily could have withstood the systemwide bank run that began after the collapse of Lehman Brothers. But what then? All three banks had significant funding needs in 2009, and asset quality had begun to deteriorate in Iceland and in operations abroad. For them, as for everyone, investment banking is a dead, or at best dormant business concept for the foreseeable future.

Icelandic banking probably had reached a point of no return by 2008, since it had not unloaded some of the weight of its assets in the prior months. Glitnir, at least, was a dead bank walking, and should have been restructured early in the year via a government-assisted merger. Kaupthing and Landsbanki both needed to deleverage aggressively by selling off foreign subsidiaries. This would have entailed major losses for their shareholders and the writing off of their shares' value. Most of the large, leveraged investment companies were also bound to be wiped out.

So deleveraging was inevitable; the question is whether the Icelanders could have been orderly about it. The banks would have needed new capital from the government, and perhaps bondholders would have agreed to turn debts into equity, at the cost of some financial institutions defaulting. In this regard, time would have been working for the Icelanders had they withstood the backlash from the Lehman collapse, after which the attitude of the international financial community toward debt restructuring would drastically change and the lenders of the Icelandic banks would probably have been cooperative, given how much they stood to lose from a default. All this was doable, provided the republic had sufficient foreign reserves to ensure the system's credibility; the banks meanwhile would have had to accumulate more foreign retail deposits and then buy back their own bonds. An unpleasant, tricky business perhaps, but anything would have been preferable to systematic collapse, for both bondholders as well as the population at large.

Speculation aside, the Icelandic government, which secured no foreign reserves and had no solutions, bears a heavy responsibility. True, three key central banks had washed their hands of the country, but there were still options available to the governing authorities. They could have bitten the bullet and obtained the foreign funds with a major bond issue in mid-2008, expensive as that option would have been. They also could have solicited the IMF for assistance, to be sure an unpleasant option and even one of last resort, since IMF loans are granted only under stringent conditions that compromise the sovereignty of the nations they aid. Iceland's political leadership was hesitant to engage the IMF and deal a blow to national pride: Iceland was an *advanced* country, after all, not a fledgling state. But stringency, however painful, might have drawn the outline for a credible plan to deleverage the nation. Painful decisions needed leadership, but that was not forthcoming: the prime minister lacked the decisiveness and the central bank governor the credibility.

As it turned out, doing nothing in the face of danger was the most reckless behavior imaginable.

CHAPTER 7

THE DOWNFALL

⇥ A CRUCIAL WEEKEND ⇤

By the first days of October, the old prime minister's residence in Reykjavik had become a bunker. Although the large, classical villa was too ornate to look the part—filled with large windows and engraved decorations, it had been built by a Norwegian whaling merchant on the western part of the island and then moved to Reykjavik in 1904 as a gift to the first prime minister of Iceland—it nonetheless had become the crisis headquarters of the nation. On Thursday and Friday, October 2 and 3, practically every Icelandic leader was seen hurrying into the building: these included labor union representatives, business leaders, investment bankers, pension fund managers, central bankers, lawyers, economists, and every politician who counted.

Outside, news anchors and foreign correspondents tried to extract comments from anyone entering or exiting the residence. As if the gloomy situation needed enhancement, an autumn chill and a pounding rainstorm were now punishing the media representatives as they kept their vigil; Prime Minister Haarde felt so sorry for them that he called in a bus to provide a bit of shelter. Downtown Reykjavik was all but abandoned. The entire nation sat in their homes, eyes fixated on TV sets and computer screens, anxious for any new headline.

The collapse of Lehman Brothers and a botched attempt to nationalize Glitnir had brought on a systemwide crisis that made all the preceding trauma to the financial sector look like a warm-up. Quite simply, the country had not faced a graver test since it had established its independence.

Evidence of panic was ubiquitous. The population feared losing not just its access to wealth but also to any haven where it might not be destroyed. Lines formed outside every Reykjavik bank as people withdrew their cash. The sight of an elderly woman walking home with plastic bags stuffed with money notes was not uncommon. Branch managers could only pray for the clocks to accelerate toward the four o'clock closing hour; many had resorted to rationing their note supply; their supply was now at less than 25 percent of capacity. Even the central bank was scraping the bottom of the barrel for paper; very few of the largest denomination, the 5,000-krona note, were left. Fresh krona notes were being printed abroad, but it would take time for this emergency supply to be flown to the island.

The currency market had also closed. Small riots had broken out on the eastern edge of the island when Polish workers collecting their wages from a local bank were denied payments in euros. Police and fire brigades had been required to restore order.

Grocery stores were jammed with hoarders who expected that the republic would soon be too short of foreign reserves to import necessities. Some residents, desperate to find shelters for their money, bought up luxury items such as rare wines, cognac, Rolex watches, even apartments. Not surprisingly, grocery chains welcomed the onrush of business; the message "Stock up at Bónus" ran in all media that first October weekend. (Many found such opportunism tasteless since the Bónus chain was owned by the infamous Jón Ásgeir Jóhannesson, also the largest owner of Baugur Group and Glitnir). One blogger compared the frenetic scene to "the day before nuclear winter."

This all was just a snapshot from the island. Abroad, runs had begun on the holdings of Icelandic banks as other financial institutions sought to close all trading lines to them and, in effect, withdraw their liquidity. The CDS spreads on Kaupthing and Glitnir now stood around 2,500 points above Libor, while Landsbanki had shot to 3,000. Their bonds were now trading on the expectation of default.

⇥ A RUN FOR THE DIGITAL AGE ⇤

At the beginning of the week, on September 29, there were about £4.7 billion in 300,000 UK Icesave accounts; by Friday some £200 million had run off. The British authorities, remembering the Northern Rock debacle of the year before, kept alert watch over the action. Landsbanki had already shifted funds to cover the UK withdrawals, but on Friday British regulators demanded that the bank transfer £400 million more directly to the Bank of England.

That same day the European Central Bank placed a margin call on Landsbanki's collateralized lending in Luxembourg, and threatened to eject all Icelandic assets unless the bank delivered cash. Glitnir also was hit with an ECB margin call, but since it had virtually no Internet deposits it had the cold comfort of knowing there was no threat of a run abroad.

The Internet's benefit to banking customers—24-hour access to transactions—now became a sledgehammer that shattered the Icesave network. Over the weekend the British press published a raft of headlines proclaiming doomsday for Iceland, and before they finished their breakfasts on Saturday Icesave customers were logging on to withdraw their money. About £300 million were pulled out that day, even while the overloaded system was stricken with "technical" difficulties that either delayed or hindered the withdrawals, a situation that evoked further howls of media outrage. Landsbanki had already requested a EUR 500 million emergency loan from CBI; without it, it was inconceivable that the bank could withstand the liquidity demands.

UK withdrawals had also spiked in Kaupthing Edge accounts that week, but on a much smaller scale, since these accounts were backed up by a British deposit guarantee (similar to the FDIC guarantee in the United States) rather than an Icelandic one, as was the case with Icesave. Edge was a diverse network, with about EUR 5.2 billion in 330,000 accounts and 11 countries. But the salacious Icesave headlines and increasing furor over its "slow" Web site were beginning to affect it as well.

British authorities were not happy with Kaupthing, either. On that first busy Friday in October, the chancellor of the exchequer, Alastair Darling, called Geir Haarde and angrily claimed that the bank was transferring money out of Britain through Kaupthing Singer & Friedlander (KSF) and back into Iceland. It was the first time the two men had ever spoken to each other directly. Darling could hardly be blamed for his testiness: a substantial transfer of UK funds into the United States had preceded the Lehman Brothers collapse just weeks before—but his accusation was incorrect. Kaupthing in cooperation with the Icelandic FSA straightened out the matter with the British over the weekend, but political leaders continued to regard all Icelandic finance with suspicion.

Unease and wariness of the coming week's events were rampant inside Kaupthing. It was selling off assets and searching out buyers for its Scandinavian operations as the desperate hustle for liquidity continued. That weekend, Einarsson asked CBI for EUR 500 million.

The consequences of letting the banks fail were being faced at last, and without exception they were grave. International law dictated that bondholders and savers held equal claim on assets recovered from defaulted banks, with the exception of the minimum deposit guarantee pegged just above EUR 20,880. Icelandic deposits only accounted for roughly 20 to 30 percent of the banks' funding, and the amount recovered on deposits above the minimum deposit guarantee after a default might be low. This was a doubly grievous situation: not only could the lion's share of the Icelandic savings pool inside the banks be wiped out, or nearly so, its remnants would be frozen in the defaulted estates until asset recovery was complete. Meanwhile, creditors would take control of the banks, which nearly meant taking control of the whole country.

About 70 percent of corporate debt in Iceland was in foreign currency. Figuring in 80 percent depreciation of the ISK and a sky-high credit premium on everything Icelandic, this meant that the majority of the companies on the island were technically bankrupt and at the mercy of the banks. Even worse, bank failures would mean the unraveling of the payment and clearing system, which would grind the entire economy to a halt.

Nor was the government insulated from the financial fallout. If it wanted to bolster confidence in the banks, by issuing a blanket guarantee on deposits, for instance, by European regulation it was required to offer the same deal to foreigners covered by the Icelandic deposit guarantee. Such deposits amounted to about 80 percent of Iceland's GDP. Collapsing banks would not only send the country reeling back into the financial Stone Age, it would instigate a government debt crisis.

⇥ THE SOLUTION ⇤

There is an old Icelandic saying with origins in the poverty- and famine-stricken past: "Iceland's misfortune carries all weapons in its grip" (Íslands óhamingju verður allt að vopni). It certainly rang true on Saturday, October 4, 2008, when the country's leaders gathered to assess their options in the face of what seemed to be the worst-case scenario brought to life. Everyone knew that a plan had to be in action before the banks reopened for business on Monday. The survival of the country seemed to be at stake.

The leaders hoped to scrape together a rescue package worth about EUR 10 billion in aid from foreign allies, government borrowing, and the sale of the national nest egg: the foreign assets of the pension funds. These foreign assets accounted for roughly 40 percent of the total pensions, the equivalent of $8 billion to $10 billion. The funds were willing to sell off about half of these holdings in exchange for Icelandic government securities and bring the currency home to shore up the foreign reserves.

Labor unions were ready to accept a wage freeze amid double-digit inflation and effectively lower their workers' purchasing power, but they also stirred the pot by insisting that the country drop its outlier stance and join the EU. The Independence Party representatives stood fast against that option. This contained ruckus notwithstanding, all interests in the country stood ready to contribute almost everything they had in an effort to solve the problem of the banks and make good on obligations abroad.

The bank CEOs checked in regularly in order to give updates on their positions and continue to press the case for emergency lending and possible restructuring of the industry. Landsbanki also lobbied for the government to issue a blanket guarantee for all Icelandic bank deposits, similar to what Ireland had done the week before in a move to stanch the flow of Icesave withdrawals. Various merger plans were floated, but each one was deemed to be either unrealistic or a political impossibility. Glitnir's demise was common to these plans, the agreed-on method of execution being its submitting to either being divided by Landsbanki and Kaupthing or being swallowed whole by Kaupthing. Landsbanki even suggested that it merge with Kaupthing. But any solution, however creative, would likely have come too late to have any bearing on the crisis with the exception of one that was backed up by huge amounts of state liquidity in hard currency.

As Saturday evening approached, it became clear that the government would not receive the foreign help that was the crux of any solution so far considered. The central banks and governments of the Western world were all hurriedly pumping liquidity into their own vulnerable financial systems. Iceland was the only Western European nation without a line to the U.S. Federal Reserve, and it was going to stay that way. For their part, the ECB and the Bank of England actually were *demanding* liquidity from Iceland, instead of offering it.

The stance taken by the big three made the smaller, Scandinavian central banks reluctant to commit themselves any further than they already had. In any financial sense, the world beyond the oceans had disappeared. Although its government was still almost debt free in foreign currency, there remained no balance of credit for, or confidence in, Iceland in any private market or national bank. Only a secret inquiry—to Russia—elicited anything approaching a positive response, although even here there was nothing approximating money in hand.

Another desperate measure was being doped out in the back rooms: Iceland could attempt to grant herself the emergency right to break international and domestic laws governing the bankruptcy proceedings of financial institutions. The notion that "necessity breaks the law," or force majeure, has a foundation in the constitutions of most Western countries. There was even a precedent in Iceland, which had invoked its emergency right during World War II, when Denmark was occupied by the Nazis, and had unilaterally cut its last ties to the Danish king and chosen its own head of state. This was drastic action usually appropriate for circumstances created by war or natural disasters, but the immediate crisis seemed equally dire, with the fate of the nation in the balance.

Just a week and a half before, on September 25, the U.S. FDIC had used its powers to seize major operating assets and liabilities of Washington Mutual and sell them to JP Morgan to bail out depositors. This left WaMu bondholders stranded with almost no recovery of their assets, but all depositors were saved. If the Americans can, the thinking went, why can't we?

Sometime between Saturday night and Sunday morning, a plurality of the government seemed to move in favor of this emergency measure. Throughout the weekend, a select group of regulators and lawyers busied themselves writing laws to support what eventually would be called "the wall of shields around Icelandic savers and homes."

On Sunday, it appeared to those outside the residence that the government was tied up in negotiations with the unions and pension funds, but this was now a smokescreen. The reporters were becoming restless, and impatient with the loud silence, since the nation was waiting for nothing less than the key to its salvation. They were more aggressive than ever when trying to extract comments from officials who passed by their ranks, going to or from the residence. By late afternoon, various unsubstantiated rumors or wishful thinking—the ECB was finally stepping in with a EUR 4 billion loan; Iceland would fast-track into the EU—were spinning out and cross-pollinating. Haarde did hold a short press conference at 6 p.m., and promised to play his hand before the markets opened the next morning, but otherwise he was evasive.

This was also the day of reckoning for the banks. The government had no choice but to pick a winner and support it, but who would it be? Landsbanki had glimmers of hope. The ECB and the British FSA, both loathe to be blamed for pulling the trigger on a major bank, had backed away from their earlier moves. The ECB had withdrawn its margin call, and the British FSA was reducing its demand for Icesave protection to £200 million, down from £400 million. The FSA even dangled the possibility of covering Icesave with a British deposit guarantee, rather in the manner of throwing a barrel over a naked man. (To this day, it is still debated in Iceland if this offer was genuine or merely a means to goad the bank into paying up.) These facts gave Landsbanki its best shot at winning the emergency loan lottery, but it fell short; Kaupthing pled its case and won.

At 11 p.m., Haarde at last invited journalists into the old prime minister's residence for the press conference all had been waiting for. His statement stunned the nation.

"This weekend has delivered such good results that no special action is needed," said Haarde. When the incredulous reporters pressed him, he quickly recoiled and declared that he needed rest. "I haven't really had a decent breakfast yet," he claimed, delivering an anticlimax for the ages. Many Icelanders could never forgive the prime minister for committing such a rank understatement and in light of later events his credibility was dealt a fatal blow.

The journalists filed out, but on a hunch most moved back into their old stakeout position. A little past midnight a taxi stopped in front of the residence. Out of it stepped suited Americans, financial experts from JP Morgan who had handled the WaMu takeover ten days before. Now they hurried inside to meet with the government of Iceland. The last details of the plan were being laid out and the "wall of shields" was being raised around Iceland.

⇥ DESPERATE BANKS, AND A BUNGLED TAKEOVER ⇤

The systemwide run on Icelandic finance was touched off by the Lehman Brothers collapse on September 15. Just as it was for Bear Stearns in March, Lehman had lost the market's confidence after posting its biggest loss ever, in the wake of rumors that it was vitally exposed to toxic real estate assets; as with any bank forsaken by the market, the subsequent liquidity run was inevitable.

This time, however, U.S. regulators had determined that there would be no government bailout and that taxpayers would not assume the burden of Lehman's bad assets to facilitate a sale. Thirty prominent executives had convened at the Fed's New York office on the weekend of September 13–14 to hammer out an alternate fix, but they could not agree on a solution. Lehman went into bankruptcy on Monday.

The regulators had a moral hazard in mind during this action. They believed they could confine this car wreck to Wall Street; the populace of Main Street could rubberneck as it chose, but it would be insulated from the damage. Lehman's default was huge, to be sure—six times greater than any previous U.S. corporate default—but it did not have any branches or depositors. It was not, by this logic, too big to fail.

Quite simply, this decision is now regarded as a cataclysmic mistake, perhaps the turning point at which the financial crisis became global. True, Lehman did not have deposits. But it had issued bonds that were sitting in money market funds all over the world; the instant reaction to the news of the collapse was a run on these funds. The bank's tentacles, its counterparty status in trades around the world, the volume of which was gigantic, were now compromised. Most trades, even those slated for "immediate delivery," actually are settled in two or three days; this meant that most of Lehman's deals from the tail end of its last week were frozen by the default, and remained frozen for weeks to come. Now every contract Lehman had entered was essentially void, trapped inside its carcass. "Counterparty risk" was now a term laden with frightening consequence: you really could lose your money just by entering a transaction with a bank that was not on secure footing. It turned out that Lehman in fact was far too interconnected to fail.

Trust among financial institutions, which had been shaky for months, evaporated. The world's payment, trading, and clearing system, a crystalline, complex web, fell to pieces after Lehman's collapse and has yet to be repaired. Iceland would be among the first to learn of this fact's dire implications.

As it turned out, the Lehman bankruptcy was just the beginning of a week that changed everything. The next day, AIG Insurance was nationalized, which led to a "Black Wednesday" on the credit markets. Lehman's disease proved contagious on both sides of the Atlantic, where money markets were in meltdown. U.S. authorities rushed to put together a rescue packet, entailing governmental absorption of "rotten" assets—mainly financial instruments tied up in subprime mortgages—and a fire-hose application of liquidity.

In Iceland, the banks had small exposure to Lehman (around EUR 180 million), but they were certain to lose more as a result of the markets' volatility. By Thursday, their CDS spreads had risen 400 points to 1,000 points above Libor, and the ISK had also taken a hit. But Friday's events brought some comfort: news of the U.S. rescue package beefed up the ISK by 3 percent, while the CDS spread narrowed by 100 points. The country also stood to gain from U.S. SEC actions to combat short selling, which had been introduced on September 17 and quickly were emulated in Europe.

"U.S. Plan Lifts Iceland" was the title of a Dow Jones Newswire report on Friday, September 19. Economists at Scandinavian Danske Bank and Nordea stated that they expected Iceland and other small, leveraged countries to be "the biggest beneficiaries" of the systemwide emergency liquidity measures. These were no more than notable instances of unfounded optimism: remember that the major central banks already had decided that Iceland was not on their list for liquidity assistance.

On September 24, the Fed announced $30 billion in swaps with four central banks—in Australia, Denmark, Sweden, and Norway—to address "elevated pressures" in their currency markets. Iceland's omission from this list was eye-catching, since it was now the only Western European nation without a line to the Fed. What was more, the Fed continued to offer these lines around the globe, but officials at CBI learned about this seemingly open invitation through the newspapers. When a request was made, CBI was flatly refused.

This put CBI in a public bind, since it would be devastating to admit to this rejection. At first, many in Iceland's market thought the Fed had simply "forgotten" about Iceland and blamed the CBI for botching the negotiation. But as another weekend approached, it became obvious that there had been no negotiation at all; the country's isolation was now almost total. The ISK market effectively froze in the days that followed, since the krona had no bidders. Banks were reduced to small, essential trades that facilitated the purchase of food, medical supplies, and gasoline. It looked like the beginning of the end.

In theory, the banks had kept very liquid balance sheets, since their assets had short maturity profiles. The catch was that a great many of those assets were either Icelandic or currency-linked loans made out to Icelandic parties; their liquidity was contingent upon their convertibility into foreign currency and, therefore, on a functioning currency market. Thus, the market freeze, coupled with the Fed's silence, rendered all banking assets effectively illiquid while the CBI could only watch helplessly.

Large reserve currencies such as the euro and dollar are always more liquid than small currencies, which means that in financial panics the small fry inevitably suffers as money rushes toward security.

It follows that in "small" currency areas, currency and banking crises are twin sisters, the former preceding the latter. The Fed's swap facilities were meant to prevent freezes in currency markets and the subsequent illiquidity of banking assets. Denied this solution, there were only two funding options left to the Icelandic banks: through retail deposits or collateralized lending from the CBI.

As stated, the funding circumstances of the three banks differed greatly at this time. Kaupthing may have entered the crisis in a compromised position in the beginning, but during 2008 the bank had truly shown its adaptability by being able to strengthen its funding position substantially and was by far the best positioned among the three banks. The bank had no large loan payments due before spring 2009, Edge accounts delivering EUR 800 million in fresh funds each month and a deposit-to-loan ratio of 50 percent. It actually benefited when savers, running for cover, moved money market funds into government-guaranteed retail savings accounts. Between 60 and 70 percent of the Edge's inflow came from Kaupthing Singer & Friedlander. In mid-September, KSF was flush, with more that £1 billion in deposits with the Bank of England.

Einarsson's stated position after the collapse confirms that the bank had felt secure enough in its liquidity to tackle speculators head-on once CDS spreads rose again in late August. In September, Kaupthing was preparing a large buyback of its own bonds, in cooperation with Deutsche Bank, and lending key customers substantial funds with which to go long against the bank in the CDS market. As for lending to private customers, this move was later criticized as smacking of favoritism and proof of shaky risk management.

On September 22, the bank announced that His Highness Sheikh Mohammed Bin Khalifa Al-Thani, of Qatar's royal family, had purchased a 5.01 percent stake for $285 million and become its third-largest shareholder. This news was well received abroad, as the royal family was known for prudent management of its interests. Questions have since been raised about the structure of the deal, but His

Highness seems to have issued a personal guarantee of about €150 million. Otherwise the funding was provided by Kaupthing.

Landsbanki was in a more compromised position. In May it had begun working with the British FSA to transfer Icesave accounts into the London-based Heritable Bank—a Landsbanki holding—and thus cover those accounts with the British guarantee on deposits. Negotiations proceeded that summer under a gentleman's agreement that asked Landsbanki not to hustle for new deposits through advertising or the offer of high rates; increasing Internet competition helped to keep Icesave's total balance stationary. But the negotiations proved fruitless, and Landsbanki's management has since complained of FSA inflexibility and increasing demands.

There were many practical difficulties attached to such a transfer. Most of the banking bonds had some kind of pari passu covenants attached that placed limitations on the size of asset transfers into subsidiaries. A breach of these covenants would have led to early redemption demands on important parts of the bank's funding. Furthermore, Landsbanki's British subsidiary, Heritable Bank, was too small to take on large loan exposure. Whatever the root cause was, by the time Lehman collapsed Icesave accounts were still the concern of the deposit guarantee of Icelandic banks, a critical detail in the events that followed.

The critical legal issues pertaining to Icelandic Internet accounts hinged on whether they were kept in a subsidiary, like Kaupthing Edge in Singer & Friedlander, or in branches, like Icesave accounts. A subsidiary is a legal entity in its own right and receives its banking license from the host country (in this case Britain); a branch is an integral legal part of the bank in the home country. In practice, EEA banking groups with cross-border operations often have centralized credit, liquidity, and risk management strategies and policies, quite regardless of whether their foreign units are branches or subsidiaries. There is a big difference, however, from the supervisory point of view. The host country has legal right to supervise subsidiaries, while branches are under the jurisdiction of the home country, with three major exceptions: financial crime, customer protection, and liquidity supervision. Consequently, host authorities can supervise branches' liquidity risks in cooperation with the home regulator.

In practice, the approach of British authorities to the accounts seems to have been much more hands-on than that of their Icelandic counterparts. They closely monitored them through the liquidity supervision. In hindsight, the contest over the Icesave accounts looks almost like a private affair between Landsbanki and the British authorities, while the Icelandic authorities, the party actually responsible for the deposit guarantee, lurked on the sidelines.

Neither party directly involved in the negotiation seems to have felt any urge for a quick resolution. The transfer of the accounts into a subsidiary would have presented severe operational challenges to Landsbanki, and the British authorities seem not to have pressed the issue. Nevertheless, sources within the Icelandic FSA and Landsbanki claimed in September 2008 that a solution to the issue was close, even just a month away. The British authorities were getting worried about the systematic risk the Icesave accounts might pose if UK savers began to question the Icelandic deposit guarantee. Furthermore, at some point they must have felt the need to protect their own savers by cooperating with Icelandic authorities. However, when the crisis hit Iceland after the fall of Lehman and the botched takeover of Glitnir, the British authorities seemed to have just changed tactics. Instead of seeking cooperation they started to use their powers as liquidity supervisors to demand funds from both Landsbanki and make the Icelandic government make good on its legal obligations.

The mitigating details for the Landsbanki funding situation in the autumn of 2008 were a comfortable EUR 800 million liquidity buffer, and the bank also had low loan redemptions until 2009. Furthermore, the Icesave accounts were opened in Holland in May and had delivered about EUR 1.7 billion since opening. Later on, the Icelandic FSA would be criticized for allowing Landsbanki to enter

Holland with an Icelandic deposit guarantee while negotiations were ongoing in Britain to move Icesave under British jurisdiction. The Icelandic FSA on the other hand stressed that Landsbanki had actually obtained the permit to open the Icesave accounts in Holland about 8 months earlier, in the autumn of 2007, and that there were really no legal grounds to stop the bank in 2008. But there was more bad news on the equity side, since a number of multinational corporate expansion projects undertaken by the bank's owners were souring and creating potential loan losses.

Primary owner Thor Björgólfsson was actively trying to shield and restructure the bank. When XL Leisure, a British travel group, collapsed on September 12 with a potential loss of EUR 207 million, Björgólfsson gave Landsbanki a personal guarantee for the loss. Also the owner of a controlling share of Straumur-Burdaras (STRB), an Icelandic investment bank with a 25 percent equity ratio and its own large balance sheet, he considered a merger of the two banks, which could deliver equity to Landsbanki and funding to STRB. But pari passu covenants complicated this maneuver as well. Landsbanki ended up selling most of its foreign subsidiaries to STRB on September 30 to free up capital; led by William Fall, an experienced British banker, STRB outlived Landsbanki by six months. Glitnir, on the other hand, was facing liquidity problems that became ever more pressing as 2008 wore on. Although the smallest of the three banks, Glitnir had the most front-loaded maturity profile on its debts, had about 1.5 billion Euros coming due by April 2009, and had not been able to fully spell out, at least not publicly, how this refinancing would be met. As noted, its Internet retail deposit arm, called Save & Save, was weak and Glitnir's owners were also the most troubled; these were heavily leveraged investment companies that needed the bank to buoy them after heavy losses in the equity market and a series of margin calls from foreign banks. Kaupthing and Landsbanki had also provided liquidity support to their owners, but unlike them, Glitnir could hardly carry the burden.

FL Group, headed up by jingle and TV comic fodder Hannes Smárason, had held a 30 percent stake until it collapsed in late 2007. FL was rescued and taken over by none other than the Baugur Group and outfitted as a holding company called Stodir. So it was that "street hooligan" Jón Ásgeir Jóhannesson became the leading owner of Glitnir. Stodir's funding, however, came chiefly from Landsbanki.

During late summer 2008, Glitnir's management focused on selling assets, mostly in Norway, and preparing asset bundles to be used in collateralized lending with the ECB. Their primary Norwegian bank holdings could not be sold, however, since rating agencies made it clear that the result would be a downgrade of operations at home. Nonetheless, Glitnir was confident it could meet its October 15 obligations, until the Lehman collapse and money market fund meltdown. After that, with all assets frozen, the bank was high and dry, with no retail funding to fall back on.

Worse, on September 24, the German Bayerische Landesbank announced that an agreement that extended a EUR 150 million loan, also due on the fifteenth, would be annulled. The stated reason was that the German bank had granted the CBI a loan a few weeks earlier, which had filled out its Icelandic quota. With that, an integral piece of Glitnir's survival strategy vanished, and its hopes of fulfilling the October obligations, given the preceding week's bad news, were dealt a death blow.

"The CBI stole our line" was a common Glitnir complaint in the aftermath, which adds irony to the events leading up to collapse. On October 24, Glitnir's board decided to solicit CBI for an emergency loan. Jóhannesson, suspicious of his old foe Governor Oddsson, was opposed, but Glitnir's board chairman, Thorsteinn Már Baldvinsson, owner of the largest fishing company in Iceland and a respected businessman in his own right, was granted a private meeting with Oddsson the next day. Faced with this more palatable representative, Oddsson was sympathetic yet noncommittal. Bad news from the United States—the collapse of WaMu—had boiled up again. On Friday, the twenty-sixth, Baldvinsson returned to CBI with Glitnir's

CEO, Lárus Welding, in tow, and this time met with the board of governors. Their loan request for EUR 600 million equaled no less than one-third of CBI's foreign reserves. Still, the governors did not tip their hand, even after Welding sent an overview of the collateral he would offer in exchange for the loan.

Later, Oddsson declared publicly that granting this request would have been "ridiculous." Over the weekend, the CBI hatched its own plan for solving Glitnir's problems.

That week, Geir Haarde and the minister of foreign affairs, Ingibjörg Sólrún Gísladóttir, were in New York to advocate for Iceland's membership on the United Nations Security Council. It was either an act of hubris by a self-important micronation or a genuine wish to help change the world; either way, the move was a break from the position of the previous tenant of the foreign ministry, Oddsson, who had all but canceled the idea. In any event, this was a curious gambit in the game of diplomacy for heads of government whose island was sinking into the Atlantic. While the board of Glitnir held an emergency meeting in Reykjavik on Wednesday, Haarde rang the closing bell at the Nasdaq.

Glitnir's precarious position chased Haarde back to Iceland, but Gísladóttir, diagnosed with a brain tumor, stayed behind for an immediate operation. Her absence proved significant in the coming days. An outspoken feminist, she was the strong-willed and undisputed leader of the Social Democrats, the second-largest political party. She had been Oddsson's main adversary for many years, and it was much to his dismay that Haarde formed a coalition government with the Social Democrats in 2007. Gísladóttir's close ties to Haarde formed the bedrock for a new government apparatus, but she was the only minister in her party who had been privy to the true details of the banking problem. Without her, the Social Democrats were all but leaderless, which for many meant that the government at large was deprived of a rudder.

On Saturday, September 27, TV reporters noticed that the traffic of officials streaming among the CBI, the ministry of finance, and the prime ministry had spiked. When the media collared Haarde, he denied that anything serious was afoot; he was just "catching up on things" after his U.S. visit. By Sunday, Kaupthing and Landsbanki had gotten wind of plans being hatched inside the CBI. Both made their final desperate attempts to intervene—Landsbanki even offered to merge with Glitnir in partnership with the government and the two banks had even started serious negotiation on the merger—but to no avail. At 10:30 p.m. on Sunday, Baldvinsson and Welding, along with their lawyers, were called to a meeting at the CBI after two days of being rebuffed or ignored. As they arrived at the bank, surrounded by camera flashes and reporters, Welding told Baldvinsson, "You know, it is all over."

Inside, Oddsson announced his terms. The EUR 600 million was available, but not as a loan; it was equity, for a 75 percent controlling stake. This meant that, effective immediately, shareholders would lose 88 percent of their current value. Glitnir had until the following morning to accept.

After this exchange, the opposition party's leaders were called to the CBI to be advised of the proposed contract. A bit after midnight, the CBI's underground garage was opened and a car emerged: a media dream. Oddsson was driving, Haarde occupied the front passenger seat and the finance minister, Árni Matthiesen, sat in the back. A photo of the car appeared on the front page of the newspapers in the morning to inform the nation that Oddsson once again held the steering wheel.

Glitnir, its dirty laundry now visible to all, was out of options. Oddsson himself declared in a press conference that morning that without CBI's assistance the bank was doomed. Glitnir's owners accepted the terms, even as Jóhannesson went on to describe it in the newspapers as "the biggest bank robbery in history." He blamed the raw deal on Oddsson's personal hostility toward his enemies. As it turned out, though, the Icelandic state would renege on the contract just one week later, against the wishes of Glitnir.

All files concerning the Glitnir nationalization are still classified inside CBI. But it is clear that the central bank governors did not consult their own specialists, rating agencies, foreign central banks, or anyone inside the domestic financial community when they cooked up their plan. It can be deduced that those responsible for the nationalization believed that it would calm the markets and boost confidence while simultaneously taking care of the leveraged holding companies. The CBI seems to have expected that Glitnir's CDS spread would narrow to parity with the state's, and that funding markets would reopen as a result. As it happened, events played out in reverse: after nationalization, the sovereign spread rose to meet Glitnir's.

It may even be that CBI was considering throwing its weight behind Glitnir as a national champion, the bank the state would support while the other two were left to their own devices. What was more, a bank had now been wrested from the grasp of the reckless investment companies, and this might be the first step toward a solution to the banking crisis.

By this time, of course, nationalization was hardly an exceptional solution; there had been a number of instances of it in the United States and Europe since Lehman went down. Outside the financial sector, economists were supportive of the move, both in Iceland and abroad. Paul Krugman, for example, wrote in his blog for the *New York Times* on September 30: "Notice, by the way, that it was an equity injection rather than a purchase of bad debt; I approve."

Be that as it may, the whole affair was in fact a gross, amateurish miscalculation. Glitnir's nationalization might not have been a bad idea had it been undertaken in concert with other banks, at home and abroad, and had CBI possessed a store of foreign reserves to feed its new dependent. But it did not have those reserves. Glitnir's refinancing needs were sufficient to wipe out most of CBI's currency reserves within 12 months. Furthermore, as the independent credit research firm Credit Sights explained a week after the takeover, "the Icelandic banks problem has not really been seen as a capital problem."

Glitnir's equity ratio did rise to 14.5 percent after the capital injection, but it hardly mattered. Even a CBI statement during the nationalization concluded that "the funding position of the bank has deteriorated in the past few days." In the eyes of the markets, Glitnir had an acute funding problem, and CBI was hardly prepared to deal with it. It is also difficult to understand why the CBI chose to act so abruptly given that negotiations with the British on Icesave were yet to finish; the Internet accounts were still under an Icelandic deposit guarantee that was a central issue in any solution to the Icelandic banking crisis.

From the foreigners' perspective, the nationalization was not a credible move, and it simply helped to demonstrate the severity of Iceland's banking problem. On the same day of the announcement, all three Icelandic banks were downgraded by Fitch. Kaupthing and Landsbanki were knocked down from A- to BBB, while Glitnir plummeted from A- to BBB-. These assessments breached covenants and unleashed a wave of margin calls and closed whatever lines of credit might have remained open. Distrust of the entire sector was building up into a tsunami abroad, and the banks were now bleeding liquidity everywhere, even from their Internet savings accounts.

As if the government's work needed to smell worse, at home it was perceived as a political or personal act against Baugur, Oddsson's attempt to win a feud that had been going on for nearly a decade. Many also sensed that there had been a power grab. "I went to sleep in a democracy but awoke in monarchy," one prominent writer wrote on his Facebook page.

And there was more fallout in store for the financial system, since all three banks had lent money on the value of Glitnir's shares; all lenders now faced a wipeout or severe losses on their loans, Landsbanki especially. Glitnir's primary owners had also issued short-term corporate notes, which, sitting in money market funds (especially at Glitnir) were now effectively worthless. Far from stabilizing anything, the nationalization accelerated the loss of confidence in Iceland and sparked mass withdrawals that started at Glitnir and spread to the other two. Such was the climate leading into the last, crucial days.

⇥ THE NATION OF TERRORISTS ⇤

The emergency plan, the "wall of shields" that Icelandic regulators created with aid from JP Morgan, essentially called for Glitnir and Landsbanki to be taken into administration, not default. Their domestic and foreign operations would be severed. All Icelandic savings and loans to corporations and individuals would be transferred into new entities—"New Glitnir" and "New Landsbanki"—that would seamlessly perpetuate domestic operations. The foreign assets would be left inside the old banks and sold as a means to compensate bondholders. In due time, the value of the transferred Icelandic assets would be assessed by an outside party (this job eventually was given to Oliver Wyman and Deloitte, an international management consulting firm). Then, the new banks would issue bonds based on the fair value assessments as a means to pay the bondholders.

Separately, the government issued a blanket guarantee of all deposits in the country, but the guarantee was to be financed by the banks' own assets. Emergency law changed the order of claimants, and domestic depositors were given priority over bondholders. In its essence, this was the same method used by the FDIC to handle the failure of WaMu, only on a national scale. The bondholders would be made to bail out depositors.

Kaupthing, as the last man standing, won the champion's share of CBI's meager resources. It was granted an EUR 500 million emergency loan; its shares in the Danish bank FIH were put up as collateral. FIH had equity of about EUR 1.3 billion but the equity was unlisted. CBI would later be criticized for lending under such conditions.

After the banking collapse, it turned out that selling FIH at a price sufficient for CBI to retrieve its loan was impossible. It is an irony that, in a country where commercial banks were criticized for being far too liberal in lending against equity as collateral, the central bank seemed guilty of the same bias. The foreign currency loans offered to both Glitnir and Kaupthing were against equity. Both banks had assets that would have been much safer collateral, such as Kaupthing's Icelandic mortgages.

Kaupthing could not really claim to have "won" the game, since its competitors had been deemed hopeless: Glitnir's wholesale funding model was beyond repair, and Landsbanki was subject to a bank run that appeared to be fatal. The foreign deposit guarantee covering most Edge accounts was considered key to Kaupthing's viability. While it was the largest of the three banks, its foreign acquisitions accounted for its bulk; its Icelandic operations were actually smaller than Landsbanki's and Glitnir's, and this, too, helped keep it alive. There was a massive cleaning job in store for the loan books of each bank in the wake of the ICEX bubble burst, and with a small market share, yet greater equity, Kaupthing's mess seemed to be the most manageable. After all, Kaupthing had twice the equity of Landsbanki but only a 20 percent share in Icelandic corporate lending, compared with its rival's 40 percent share.

But here, too, there were factors that darkened even these modest forecasts. The loan book cleanup turned out to be far more extensive than anticipated, and Kaupthing surely would have needed yet another equity injection from the state to survive in the months to come. Rather than accept total destruction, it briefly seemed wiser to support Kaupthing's fighting chance and to retain a single international, private bank in Iceland.

Geir Haarde introduced this new emergency plan in a press conference on Monday, October 6, just 17 hours after he had announced that "no action" was needed. He delivered a bleak sermon that was received like a cold shower by his constituents and foreigners alike:

"Fellow countrymen . . . If there was ever a time when the Icelandic nation needed to stand together and show fortitude in the face of adversity, then this is the moment. I urge you all to guard that which is most important in the life of every one of us, to protect those values which will survive the storm now beginning. I urge families to talk together and not to allow anxiety to get the upper hand, even though the outlook is grim for many. We need to explain to our children that the world is not on the edge of a precipice, and we all need to find an inner courage to look to the future . . . Thus with Icelandic optimism, fortitude and solidarity as weapons, we will ride out the storm. God bless Iceland."

It was reported that Independence Party members of parliament responded with a standing ovation. To the rest of the populace the speech was incomprehensible.

Oddsson took a prime-time TV spot on Tuesday to pitch the "wall of shields" and strengthen the nation's resolve. His candor hardly befitted his position, perhaps the most sensitive in the nation given the situation. While a leader can hardly be faulted for attempting to bolster the hopes of his country, Oddsson's straight talk, aimed at the domestic audience, read like nuclear waste to interested parties abroad. It is worthwhile to quote a part of his interview (italics added):

David Oddsson: I think many have not quite figured out what actually is changing, everybody is terribly pessimistic as this shake-up now hits many very hard. Many are very indebted and many of those in debt owe many other innocent parties who then stand to lose money. But what are we actually doing and must we be so pessimistic? What are we doing? We have decided that we are not going to pay the foreign debts of reckless people, debts that have been. . . .

Interviewer: Why do you say reckless people?

Mr. Oddsson: Hold on, those who cannot pay were in the old days called reckless, I learned that from my grandmother, we do not intend to pay other people's debts, *we do not intend to pay the debts of the banks that have been a little heedless.* And what do I mean by that? Earlier it was believed that the Icelandic system, the Icelandic State and Icelandic taxpayers would try to pay all the debts of the Icelandic banks, and of course, when the Icelandic banks will need 50 to 55 billion euros in the next three to four years and cannot provide this amount because all the markets are closed, then we would be placing such a debt burden on our children and grandchildren that it would be slavery for other people's fault. Now we are doing the same thing the U.S. did for instance to Washington Mutual. They say that this particular player lent money to all kinds of projects that failed in the end but might have been fine if everything had been fine and dandy and no problems had arisen in the world. These players lent this money to make a profit, nothing wrong with that, and they must face the consequences and not innocent citizens. .... Many still think this is problematic, but we have made this rather drastic decision and say: we are not going to pay the banks' foreign debts.

Interviewer: This is perhaps more than a "rather drastic" move as it presumably means that we will not enjoy any trust in the world when we have written off foreign debt in . . .

Mr. Oddsson: We are not writing off the foreign debts of the State, we did exactly the same as . . .

Interviewer: No, but private parties.

Mr. Oddsson: Yes, we are doing precisely the same as the Americans are doing.

Interviewer: Is it then going to be a single Icelandic bank?

Mr. Oddsson: Well, there is one bank still operational and perhaps there will still be two other banks with domestic services, let's see what happens, let's hope for the best. But what then happens is that this foreign debt will be settled and of course it is a fact that the foreign creditors will unfortunately only get 5–10–15 percent of their claims.

Interviewer: But don't you examine the consequences of [rescuing Glitnir] and what chain of events might start afterwards because this all happened so quickly, and . . .?

Mr. Oddsson: We took a look and saw that a bank is about to fail and everybody knows the consequences of that, the risk to reputation is great and a decision was made to try and save it through public funds. And it was received with great ingratitude. I have never known more ingratitude . . .

When the banks had expanded out people started yelling that we must enlarge the foreign currency reserves in step with the banks' growth. A totally wrong theory. We should have cut the banking system down and adjust[ed] it to our needs and not those of this daredevil expansion abroad.

Interviewer: Will you continue to have confidence in the króna as a solid currency after this storm?

Mr. Oddsson: It is of course very difficult for me to discuss and defend the króna under these circumstances, but whatever people say and however heavy the criticism is, the króna is the instrument we have to work ourselves out of these difficulties and to even out the fluctuations in our society. If we were tied to the euro, for instance, we would just have to succumb to the laws of Germany and France. But I know that all spinmeisters talk that way about the króna but as soon as people think the matter through and as soon as people realize what is going on and how the króna will now help us regain our balance, this chorus will stop. That's how it will be.

Interviewer: But the State of Iceland is faltering along with [the banks], perhaps?

Mr. Oddsson: No, because we do not intend to do so. We do not intend to do so. We actually do not intend to sink with the banks, to let the public sink with the banks. That is the good news, that is the good news and the State is not broke. The State is doing very well and let's keep our heads fairly clear and do not let everybody confuse us and figure out who created this dilemma, who the arsonists were.

Interviewer: And you have no doubts about that, it is the foreign expansion people?

Mr. Oddsson: Well, what I find odd is when people feel mainly for the arsonists and attack the fire brigade.

At first it appeared that the government's plan could work. All the banks opened for business that Monday, savings were secure, and the domestic payment system was functional. Stasis was maintained even after Landsbanki was taken into administration that evening and followed by Glitnir on Tuesday; the state forfeited on the contract it had cobbled together the week before. Confidence began to return as the bank runs subsided and businesses retained their access to the new banks. Inside the banks, painful reorganization needed to be done, since the banks had to be cut down in size to match their Icelandic operations. Close to one-third of Landsbanki's 1,400 to 1,500 employees lost their jobs.

Kaupthing, its fate still in the balance, also held on, buffeted and buoyed in turn by new developments. Icesave's Web page had been shut down since the weekend, leaving its customers without a clue as to the status of their deposits. This, along with worldwide commentary on the national catastrophe, began to affect Edge accounts despite their British guarantee; the week began with heavy outflows. But on Tuesday, October 7, the Swedish central bank (Riksbank) granted an emergency loan worth about 5 billion Swedish kronor, with Kaupthing's operations in that country as collateral. The management was determined to sell down assets and hold out.

The roots of the emergency law that gave the Icelandic FSA the extraordinary powers it wielded in the banking crisis can be traced back to 2004, the very start of the Icelandic banking expansion. At that time, a special committee of high-ranking officials was tasked with formulating authoritative responses to "possible difficulties in the financial market." But it took the 2006 Geyser crisis to provide the committee with the impetus to wrap up its protracted review process;

its final report was delivered in February 2006. The report stressed the need for coordination between various administrative units and strongly recommended legislative amendments that would expand the FSA's power to intervene in the event of a banking crisis.

The report was published on the Web site of the Prime Minister's office, but not much else happened. The suggested amendments were left in limbo; they were not even submitted to Parliament in a formal legislative bill until the emergency law was passed in the midst of the crisis. The Icelandic FSA never received genuine powers of intervention in the financial market until the banks were effectively dead. Instead, there was more debate. Some argued for bringing the FSA under the authority of the CBI; this idea did have some merit, and Oddsson, as CBI governor, advocated for it publicly.

Nevertheless, the emergency law could not, as such, be considered that much of an anomaly if it had been applied just to a single institution rather than a whole financial system. In case of emergency, governments will always act on behalf of depositors no matter the cost. Clearly, there would be abundant long-term problems for everyone. The rescue plan roughed up bondholders, but there was little political sympathy in this matter. There would of course be long-term consequences, as it was uncertain (and still is, today) when Iceland would again be able to procure a foreign loan on the private market, or if the state would be hunted through litigation. The immediate urgency arose from the decision of the Icelandic authorities to allow domestic depositors to take precedence over foreign depositors. Many abroad considered this discrimination, based on nationality, which went against the principles of the European Common Market.

The government publicly insisted that it would meet its legal obligations and abide by European directives, which meant it would pay the minimum EUR 20,880 guarantee on Icesave deposits. This stance was considered ambiguous, however, since by strict definition the legal responsibility for this guarantee lay, as with all European nations, with the Depositors' and Investors' Guarantee Fund, a puddle of equity that amounted to less than 1 percent of the total deposits in Icesave. The minuscule size of the DIGF fund was in itself not an issue since it was broadly in line with other similar funds in other European countries. The issue centered on the willingness of the Icelandic government to support the fund to meet its claims. The DIGF did have priority over bondholders concerning Landsbanki's assets, but not over Icelandic deposits, which were protected by the government bailout. Still, Iceland was withholding on action that would put its taxpayers on the hook for Icesave losses abroad.

This reticence is easy to understand if a few frightening numbers are considered. Landsbanki's assets simply were considered insufficient to bail out both domestic and foreign deposits. IceSave's stake in the UK and Holland amounted to about $12 billion, or 60 percent of the national GDP, in September. When the ISK tanked the following month, the ratio ballooned to 80 percent. The minimum foreign amount due was somewhat lower—£2.35 billion in the UK and €1.33 in Holland—but even this amount represented between 40 and 60 percent of the GDP, depending on the ISK value.

It is debatable if any sovereign nation would voluntarily accept such high indemnity, especially if its economy was in the process of cratering. As Oddsson stated, "Placing such a debt burden on our children and grandchildren . . . would be slavery for other people's fault." Media in Iceland compared the Icesave claims with the German reparations payments made after World War I that sucked out 85 percent of that nation's GDP and turned its postwar economy into a ruin with hyperinflation. It seemed grossly unfair that the same countries who had ignored desperate calls for help now demanded payment in the wake of disaster.

Across the Atlantic, Britain was reeling from its own troubles. Despite a population 200 times that of Iceland, the UK was in a similar plight; like Iceland, it had an open economy, its own currency, an oversized international banking system, and shaken confidence in its financial system. There were many British banks in dire straits, and they and the government had held emergency meetings of their own all through the weekend. Prime Minister Gordon Brown was taking fire for not containing the crisis, and the ruling Labour Party's approval ratings had dropped to their lowest point in 20 years.

There were 300,000 Icesave account holders in the nation: these included prominent charities, hospitals, municipalities, universities, the London police, pensions, and thousands of private citizens. They wanted their money back, pure and simple, and the government had little choice but to pursue the matter or further jeopardize confidence in their own the financial sector and their support base.

The Icelandic government clearly was misguided to abandon Icesave depositors and allow their Internet accounts to be closed without any explanation or assurances. These were people and institutions that had trusted the good name of Iceland when they committed their savings. On the other hand, Iceland's government feared for its existence as a sovereign nation and by now had reason to believe its friendships were all of the fair-weather variety. Furthermore, it did not have the experience to combat a financial crisis. There were many Icelanders with acumen in banking, finance, and international relations, but almost without exception they were employed by the banks or the new multinationals. State institutions, until now defined as having an inward, domestic scope, had an international situation to handle, and they proved to be overmatched.

It is still unclear just how much the governments of Iceland and Britain communicated that October. It is known that Gordon Brown and Geir Haarde spoke over the crucial weekend, as did Oddsson and his British counterpart, Mervin King. The contents of these conversations are still classified. If there is any substance to the prevailing rumors, Iceland probably deserves blame for not showing its hand and seeking immediate cooperation after passing its emergency law.

But if Britain was inclined to cooperate, at the least they can be faulted for being either tardy or oblivious to certain possibilities. Talks concerning Icesave and British jurisdiction had been ongoing for months. When the run drained Landsbanki of its domestic currency reserves and threatened worse, the British authorities stood on the sidelines. Over the crucial weekend, they finally considered fast-tracking Icesave under British guarantee if the Icelandic government simultaneously granted an emergency loan, a response that was either hopelessly belated or a fig leaf. Meanwhile, Kaupthing/Singer & Friedlander was offered no assistance at all, even though it had collateral and already had received assistance from both Iceland and Sweden. It is simply difficult to find any evidence that the British political leadership was in fact seeking any cooperation at all. On the contrary, the evidence seems to be that they were hatching out their own solution that had been some time in the making.

The optimal solution would have been for the two governments to cooperate and issue some kind of a joint guarantee of the Icesave deposits. Actually, the Financial Services Compensation Scheme guaranteed £35,000 for all banks in Britain. If the bank was foreign, operating under the European Economic Area "passport" system, the host country would pay the minimum £16,300 with the FSCS picking up the balance. Ironically, the FSCS raised its guarantee level from £35,000 to £50,000 on the very day that Landsbanki went into default. This did not affect the liability of the Icelandic deposit guarantee under the passport system, but it automatically increased the cost to British authorities when Landsbanki collapsed.

It would therefore seem that the British had abundant cause to contain the situation, especially once it was clear the Icelandic authorities were helpless and the run was leading up to a disaster. Whatever might be the fate of Landsbanki as an independent company, a joint guarantee or some other supporting measure might have stopped the run. As a bonus, Kaupthing might have been saved as well.

The funds needed for a rescue mission were quite small in relation to the possible losses in both countries. It was such a volatile time—Kaupthing Edge was also subject to a run despite its British deposit guarantee—that even the most sober and impartial methods might have been insufficient to quell the crisis.

In hindsight, it does seem that one thought was paramount with the British authorities: no assistance for Icelanders, in any form. Recall that Iceland's excursion in the country was considered to be a nuisance. Then again, perhaps the greedy depositors needed a lesson for having trusted a risk-seeking foreign bank that offered returns above market rates? Or maybe the British just had their hands full trying to save their own financial system and weren't able to give much attention to the Icelanders.

Whatever the explanation, while Iceland threw together its emergency plan the British political leadership seemed to be fixated on their own plan. On October 7, Finance Minister Darling called his Icelandic counterpart Árni Matthiesen.

THE CONVERSATION BETWEEN ALASTAIR DARLING AND ÁRNI MATTHIESEN ON TUESDAY MORNING, OCTOBER 7 2008.

Matthiesen: Hello.

Darling: Hello.

Matthiesen: This is Árni Matthiesen, Minister of Finance.

Darling: Hello, we met a few months ago, weeks ago.

Matthiesen: No, we have never met. You met the Minister of Trade.

Darling: Alright, sorry.

Matthiesen: No problem.

Darling: Thank you for taking the call. As you know, we have a huge problem with Landsbanki, we have a branch here, which has got four billion pounds worth of deposits and it has now been shut and I need to know exactly what you are doing in relation to it. Could you explain that to me?

Matthiesen: Yes, this was explained in a letter we sent the night before last from the Trade Ministry. Since then, we have set out a new legislation where we are prioritizing the deposits and where we are giving the FME, the Icelandic FSA authorities, the authority to go into banks, similar legislation to what you have in England, and the Landsbanki is now under the control of the FME, and they are in the process of working out how to do these things, but I think this legislation will help in solving this problem.

Darling: What about the depositors you have got who have got deposits in London branches?

Matthiesen: We have the insurance fund according to the Directive and how that works is explained in this letter and the pledge of support from the government to the fund.

Darling: So the entitlements the people have, which I think is about sixteen thousand pounds, they will be paid that?

Matthiesen: Well, I hope that will be the case. I cannot visibly state that or guarantee that now, but we are certainly working to solve this issue. This is something we really don't want to have hanging over us.

Darling: People are asking us already, what is happening there? When will you work that through?

Matthiesen: Well, I really can't say. But I think it is the best thing that the FSA be in close touch with the FME about this to see how the timeline works out in this.

Darling: Do I understand that you guarantee the deposits of Icelandic depositors?

Matthiesen: Yes, we guarantee the deposits in the banks and branches here in Iceland.

Darling: But not the branches outside Iceland?

Matthiesen: No, not outside of what was already in the letter that we sent.

Darling: But is that not in breach of the EEA-treaty?

Matthiesen: No, we don't think so and think this is actually in line with what other countries have been doing over recent days.

Darling: Well, we didn't when we had the problem with Northern Rock. It didn't matter where you saved money, we guaranteed your savings.

Matthiesen: Well, yes, that was actually in the beginning at least debated. I am sure you cleared that up in the end.

Darling: The problem, I do understand your problem, the problem is that you have people who put their money into a bank here and they are finding that you have decided not to look after their interests. This would be extremely damaging to Iceland in the future.

Matthiesen: Yes, we realize that and we will be trying as hard as we possibly can to make this not a problem. We are in a very, very difficult situation . . .

Darling: I can see that . . .

Matthiesen: . . . and just this week, since we can't cure the domestic situation we can't really do anything about things that are abroad. So we must first deal with the domestic situation, and then we will certainly try to do what we possibly can, and I am personally optimistic that the legislation that we passed last night will strengthen this part of it. And we, of course, realize what could happen and don't want to be in . . .

Darling: yes . . .

Matthiesen: But the point is also, Chancellor, that we have for months been trying to talk to everybody around us and trying to tell them that we were in trouble and ask them for support and we have actually gotten very little support.

Darling: I understand that, but I have to say that when I met your colleague and these others, basically, what we were told turns out not to have been right. I was very concerned about the London banking position and they kept saying there was nothing to worry about. And you know, with the position we are now in, there will be a lot of people in this country who put money in and who stand to lose an awful lot of money and they will find it difficult to understand how that has happened.

Matthiesen: Well, I hope that won't be the case. I wasn't at the meeting, so I can't say . . .

Darling: Well, I know that. Can you tell me this, if the insurance fund you refer to, does it have money to pay out?

Matthiesen: They have some money, but as is with most of these funds, it is very limited compared to the exposure.

Darling: Yeah, so you don't know. See, I need to know this, in terms of what I tell people. It is quite possible that there is not enough money in that fund. Is that right?

Matthiesen: Well, yes, that is quite possible.

Darling: Well, that is a terrible position to be in.

Matthiesen: Yes, we are in a terrible position here and the legislation we were passing through last night is an emergency legislation and, as I say, we are just trying to ensure the domestic situation so that we can then secure other situations.

Darling: What I . . . I take it therefore that the promise Landsbanki gave us, that it was going to get 200 million pounds of liquidity back into it, has gone as well.

Matthiesen: Yes, they didn't get that liquidity.

Darling: Well, you know, I do understand your position. You have to understand that the reputation of your country is going to be terrible.

Matthiesen: Yes, we do understand that. We will try our utmost to avoid that. We need to secure the domestic situation, before I can give you any guarantees for anything else.

Darling: Obviously, I would appreciate any help you can give.

Matthiesen: Obviously . . .

Darling: Sure . . . We would have to explain to people here what has happened. It will, of course, no doubt, have repercussions for others. It really is a very, very difficult situation where people thought they were covered and then they discover the insurance fund has got no money in it.

Matthiesen: Yes, as we said in the letter . . .

Darling: OK, I will appreciate whatever help you can give.

Matthiesen: Yes, we will need for the FSA and FME to be in touch on the . . .

Darling: Oh, I know they most certainly will. I know you were not at the meeting and weren't part of it. We doubted what we were being told then and I am afraid we were right.

Matthiesen: Yes, that can be.

Darling: Anyway, please keep in touch. Whatever you can do to help, that will be very helpful indeed.

Matthiesen: Yes: if there are any areas on your side, please be in touch.

Darling: Alright. I will do that. Thank you very much indeed.

Matthiesen: Thank you.

Darling: Goodbye.

Matthiesen: Bye.

Matthiesen, who was in the middle of a meeting, was totally unprepared. He did not think he was giving an official response; to him, it seemed to be an unofficial communiqué with a British colleague. He was overseeing the collapse of a financial system, sleep deprived, and haggard. It is difficult to see how his responses in that single conversation could have justified the actions that followed.

Matthiesen has since espoused his belief that Darling's phone call was no more than a means to cover for a decision that was already in place. All evidence that has surfaced in the course of the now ongoing lawsuit by Kaupthing's former shareholders points in this same direction.

When Darling was interviewed on BBC Radio on the morning of October 8, he stated:

"The Icelandic government, believe it or not, has told me yesterday they have no intention of honouring their obligations here . . . Because this is a branch of a foreign bank the first call would be on the Icelandic compensation scheme which, as far as I can see, hasn't got any money in it . . . But I have decided in these exceptional circumstances that we will stand behind those depositors so they get their money back."

Gordon Brown held a press conference at 9:15 that same morning, and unveiled his new plan for saving the British banking system with a £500 billion rescue package. There was more to report than a bailout at home, however. Brown used the opportunity to announce that he was "taking legal action against the Icelandic authorities to recover the money lost to people who deposited in UK branches of its banks."

Indeed, he was. Barely one hour later, the British government enacted an antiterrorism law (Landsbanki Freezing Order 2008) that authorized them to seize all assets of Landsbanki in Britain. The freezing order was issued under the 2001 Anti-Terrorism, Crime and Security Act, which was passed after the 9/11 attacks. The application of this law to a peaceful nation or bank that was truly not involved in terrorist activities was unprecedented. Later that day, Landsbanki, CBI, and the Icelandic finance ministry were listed with other "financially sanctioned regimes" such as Al Qaeda, the Taliban, North Korea, and Burma. (The CBI and Icelandic ministry of finance were later removed, leaving Landsbanki as the lone Icelandic bedfellow of terrorist states.)

This action probably did more to revive Brown's popularity than any other. A typical response, recorded by the BBC later that day after the statement from Darling, came from Mike Davis, age 62, who had £75,000 in retirement savings locked up in an Icesave account. Claiming that he had not slept in days, Davis said he was "highly relieved and thankful" after hearing the chancellor's pledge. "It has restored my faith in Britain and the British government." Both Brown and the Labour Party watched their approval ratings jump in next few days.

But they had more in store for Iceland than this. As a result of the negative publicity, the outflow from Kaupthing Edge had turned into a flood. On the morning of October 8, the British FSA asked Kaupthing for an additional £300 million infusion to address the deteriorating liquidity situation. Sensing that his position in Britain was now untenable, Sigurdur Einarsson asked Deutsche Bank if it would be possible to sell KSF. The Deutsche advisors thought it was quite possible, but noted that a sale would take 24 to 48 hours to complete. At 9:30 a.m., while discussing KSF sales options, Einarsson watched a headline run across his TV screen: "ING Buys 3 Billion Pounds of Deposits From Icelandic Banks." Without his knowledge, the British FSA had seized the Kaupthing Edge deposits (about $4.5 billion), sold them off to ING, and sent the KSF into bankruptcy proceedings. Landsbanki's holding, Heritable Bank, was condemned to the same fate.

Singer & Friedlander was an independent UK bank, and its bankruptcy did not automatically take down its mother company in Iceland. But it did breach Kaupthing loan covenants and open up the possibility of an early redemption for bondholders. The rest of that day was filled with frantic attempts to persuade bondholders not to request early redemption. Some agreed to waive their rights, but others, who had hedged themselves out by shorting Kaupthing in the CDS market, actually stood to gain from the default that would result.

Management gave up the ghost at midnight. Control of Kaupthing was given over to the Icelandic FSA. In three days, all of the Icelandic banking giants and 85 percent of the financial system had collapsed. Seventy-five percent of the stock market value was wiped out.

The government was in a state of shock. Apart from Darling's call to Matthiesen on Tuesday morning, there had been no discussion, and no warning of Britain's intentions. Nevertheless, Britain's treasury spokesman stated that "the UK government has made it clear repeatedly that this decision to protect UK depositors in Icelandic banks was made after extensive conversations with the Icelandic government."

Haarde held a press conference at 4 p.m., October 9, to express his personal upset and shock at the use of "hostile" antiterrorism legislation as a means to freeze the assets of Icelandic banks. Beyond that, he refused to discuss the matter publicly. Iceland's official statement toed a friendly line:

The Icelandic government appreciates that the British authorities are willing to step in and respond to the immediate concerns of depositors of Landsbanki's Icesave accounts. The governments of the two countries will immediately review the matter in detail through official channels with a view to finding a mutually satisfactory solution. It should also be highlighted that on Monday evening changes were made to the Act on the Depositors' and Investors' Guarantee Fund [that strengthened] the position of depositors by giving them priority when allocating assets. There is a good probability that the total assets of Landsbanki will be sufficient to cover the deposits in IceSave. The Icelandic government reiterates that if needed it will support The Depositors' and Investors'

Guarantee Fund in raising necessary funds. The government of Iceland is determined not to let the current financial crisis overshadow the long standing friendship between Iceland and the United Kingdom.

For his part, Gordon Brown had no objection to taking this matter public. He did not take Haarde's call on October 9. Haarde was able to speak with Darling, who assured him that transactions between their countries would return to normal. Meanwhile, Brown told BBC political editor Nick Robinson, "I've spoken to the Icelandic prime minister, I have told him this is effectively an illegal action that they have taken. We are freezing the assets of Icelandic companies in the UK where we can. We will take further action against the Icelandic authorities where necessary to recover the money."

This sounded like some kind of corporate ethnic cleansing. Brown seemed intent on confiscating the firms and assets of Icelanders who had done nothing wrong beyond standing under the same flag as the accursed banks. Later that day, Brown declared on Sky News that Iceland was bankrupt.

The gaming between Brown and Haarde turned into a contest of cat and mouse. However, Iceland's government, without an effective spokesperson or a well-placed public relations channel inside Britain, looked amateurish, short work for serious professionals.

At home and abroad, Icelanders experienced their country's "terrorist entity" label as the final tremor that brought down the house. The nation's international payment system collapsed. Funds sent to other countries were held up at some banks, or simply disappeared. Money could not be sent outside the island. Most banks simply refused either to send or to receive Icelandic payments. Icelanders throughout the world often found to their horror that their credit cards no longer worked and that they could not transfer funds from home. Foreign trade became next to impossible, since payments could not be cleared.

All at once, everything Icelandic had become toxic, untouchable, banished to a place outside the world of business. The situation in

Britain was the worst; accounts of all Icelandic businesses were effectively frozen until the British authorities at last made it clear that the freezing order pertained only to Landsbanki. Despite this single mercy, Gordon Brown had brought the Icelandic economy to its knees with a single swipe.

The cultural and personal ramifications of the invocation of the Terrorist Act were terrible as well. The Icelanders had looked up to the British and emulated many of their ways. "We thought they were our friends" was a typical, plaintive response at the outset. But public anger soon began to grow over the perceived injustice. Kicking a tiny, friendless island carried no cost for British authorities, since such tactics are still admired in many quarters. While UK street papers shouted for Icelanders to "Give us our money back," most Brits conveniently ignored that the Terrorist Act had made it harder than ever for the banks to pay.

Icelanders in Britain were told off by customs officials at airports, thrown out of rental apartments, laid off at work, and verbally abused as thieves in the pubs. They were ridiculed in other countries as well, and subjected to cheap shots. A Danish paper held a mock charity drive in Cophenhagen's main square to support penniless Icelanders. There was also some magnanimity, especially in the form of financial aid to students who were stranded by the collapse of the payment system. Perhaps the nation's risk-seeking and self-assuredness (or arrogance) warranted this comeuppance; even if this was so, the experience of a friendless world was a bitter one.

At home, CBI set to picking up the pieces. It replaced the banks and became the economy's international clearinghouse. A number of specialists from the former banks' treasury departments were enlisted for the effort. Also, JP Morgan was contracted to act as an intermediary in the payments moving in and out of the country. Over the ensuing months, the payment system was rebuilt.

CHAPTER 8

LOST IN ICELAND

⊰ FROM RUSSIA WITH LOVE ⊱

Tuesday, October 7, was a day when bank employees came early to work, even though they had no idea if their employers had a future in the world. Landsbanki had gone into receivership with the FSA the night before and Glitnir, its contract for government purchase notwithstanding, was next; Kaupthing followed on Wednesday, believing to the last that it would be the sole survivor.

The currency market were for most purposes closed—there were no buy offers for the bludgeoned ISK—but the dealers' phone lines were hot with calls from terrified foreign traders seeking to clear out their ISK positions.

But at 8:26 that morning, the CBI made an astounding announcement: "The Foreign Exchange Reserves of the Central Bank of Iceland are bolstered."

The announcement seemed to be a deus ex machina that could yank the nation away from the precipice. It declared that the Russian ambassador to Iceland, Victor I. Tatarintsev, had told CBI's chairman of the Board of Governors—David Oddsson—that very morning that Russia would grant the bank a EUR 4 billion loan. Its maturity would be three to four years, on terms in a range of 30 to 50 basis points above Libor. Prime Minister Vladimir Putin had confirmed his nation's commitment to the loan. Geir Haarde had initiated talks with Russia some months before. Representatives of the CBI and the government were to finalize the agreement in Moscow. The loan would be life-blood to CBI's foreign exchange reserves and would stabilize the krona's exchange rate.

The research departments of the banks immediately were barraged with queries from foreign analysts and reporters who wanted the inside take on what was really happening. Forty minutes later, CBI issued a second announcement titled "Foreign Exchange Measures." It stated that "following consultations with the Prime Minister, the Central Bank of Iceland has decided to engage in foreign exchange transactions in the interbank market today at an exchange rate that takes reference from the trade weighted index of 175, equivalent to 131 krónur vis-à-vis the Euro."

In other words, CBI was announcing a peg of a far more favorable exchange rate than had existed in the last market trades of the prior week. Given the lack of an active currency market in the new week—when all three banks were headed to receivership—the peg was far above any sensible market-clearing price.

There was something amiss, and confusion set in. CBI's economic department seemed paralyzed by disbelief, without information; this announcement was all news to them. Moscow officials at the ministry of finance did not seem to recognize the terms of the loan, either.

CBI had to admit that this loan had yet to be finalized. At 11:13—not quite three hours after the sensational news broke—the following quotation appeared on TV screens around the country while a cable show was airing on the Bloomberg business news network: "Central bank Governor David Oddsson said an announcement earlier today in Reykjavik that the Russian loan had been agreed upon was incorrect and talks were 'ongoing.' Russian Finance Minister Alexei Kudrin confirmed that 'we have a request from the Icelandic government' and said Russia's reaction is 'positive.'"

Given this volatile news cycle, the new peg did not fare well. The dealers at the banks instantly called CBI to buy foreign currency at the advertised price. After a brief hesitation, the bank sold off EUR 6 million. None of the banks was willing or able to give away their euros by selling them at this price, being on the way to receivership or already there. Nevertheless, CBI published a new announcement on its Web site the next morning:

"Measures designed to create stability concerning a realistic exchange rate for the króna are still in progress. . . . This does not mean that the exchange rate has been fixed; it only means that the Central Bank considers the low ISK exchange rate that has developed in the recent term unrealistic. The Bank requests that market makers in the interbank market support its attempts to strengthen the króna."

That stance was held for most of the day, until CBI pulled in its horns and published a new announcement:

"For the past two days, the Central Bank of Iceland has carried out foreign currency trading at a different exchange rate than that on the foreign exchange market. It is clear that there is insufficient support for this exchange rate; therefore, the Bank will not make any further such efforts for the time being."

This was probably the shortest peg in history, and it was an embarrassment for Icelandic economists. The aptitude—or lack thereof—of their central bank was now subject to public ridicule. A peg of this kind is useless unless it is supported by credible economic measures and ample foreign reserves. Even assuming the EUR 4 billion Russian loan was granted, it might have worsened the situation had its funds been offered to the private sector at an absurdly low price through a peg. The banks, such as they now were, retained just enough public trust to keep citizens from cleaning out their deposit accounts, but that trust was extremely fragile. It certainly was possible that opening the currency market again with a favorable conversion rate might precipitate another bank run, as people sought to convert their assets into euro notes or transfer them outside the system to foreign bank accounts.

Meanwhile, the mere possibility of Iceland accepting a Russian loan brought a new geopolitical dimension to the banking crisis, one that threatened to develop into a new international dispute. On October 10, after the failed peg attempt, CBI started to ration out foreign exchange, with preference given to trade in necessities.

⇥ THE HANGOVER FROM THE CARRY TRADE ⇤

Iceland had endured two crises in 2008. One, in banking, was "solved" by the collapse and restructuring of the three major banks. The currency crisis had actually started in March but it became acute when the krona became all but inconvertible by the end of September; the banking collapse did nothing to solve it. It peaked, at new, unprecedented heights, after Britain invoked terrorist laws on October 8, which practically cut off the currency market's payment-clearing mechanism from the rest of the world.

Repairing the payment system was slow, steady work. But the currency crisis could not be solved without an outside loan, due to a great hangover from the carry trade. CBI had fixed its policy rate at about 10 percent above that of the neighboring countries for the past three years, keeping currency high and inflation low. This attracted great quantities of hot money from abroad and contributed mightily to the disequilibrium and overheating of the Icelandic economy. Prior to the banks' demise, the speculative position of foreigners in Icelandic interest-yielding assets or derivative contracts was around ISK 1,000 billion to ISK 1,200 billion: the equivalent of 80 to 100 percent of the M3 money supply, or 70 to 80 percent of the GDP. The banking collapse automatically cleared up a great deal of this problem, since all derivative or swap contracts with the three banks were now locked up in their defaulted estates.

However, in response to a depreciating krona, Icelandic authorities had floated many large, nominal bond issues, as well as certificates of deposit at the CBI, to lure foreign funds into the country. Foreign speculators were able to obtain the high interest directly from the state without the intermediation of the banks; after the banking collapse, they had about ISK 500 billion trapped in various securities. These funds had to be released for the currency market to ever recover, and to that end foreign currency reserves were needed.

When they wheeled out their emergency law, the Icelandic authorities' primary intent was to protect the balance sheet of their debt-free republic. Taxpayers had to remain unburdened by the debts amassed by "reckless" bankers. Therefore, authorities argued, the nation was a much safer credit risk now that the bloated banking system was finished, its contingent liability evaporated.

Of course, the state was bound to honor its obligations, and it had not survived the banking crisis without being splattered with some debt. CBI had lent to the banks with their bonds as collateral—these were now effectively worthless—and there had been a government bailout of the money market funds. Now the new banks needed equity. Yet when its fiscal house was at last in order, it seemed likely the government would be no more indebted than that of any other Western nation that had bailed out its banks—perhaps less so. But then, there were the Icesave claims.

Despite the beginnings of a recovery plan, the world press customarily referred to Iceland as a bankrupt nation, much to the political leadership's annoyance. What was more, other nations were no more willing to lend than they had been before the collapse. It would have been quite fair to ask the government just what plans it had for solving the currency crisis in the event of a loan; after all, the two-day peg had not exactly bolstered its credibility. Rather than risk their own funds, other countries all pointed Iceland in the same direction, toward the International Monetary Fund.

ACCEPTING AID RELUCTANTLY

IMF assistance is an obvious solution to a currency crisis. Indeed, it might have alleviated Iceland's banking crisis as well, should the government have had the wisdom to ask before the collapse. It would not have been the first time Iceland, a founding IMF member, had requested assistance. But fear of lost sovereignty, or even foolish pride, seems to have prevented Iceland from seeking out the fund as at least a stand-by facility.

On October 3, Tryggvi Thor Herbertsson, then the economic advisor to the prime minister, was asked if he thought the nation would seek IMF aid. "We're an industrialized country, the fifth-richest country in the world per capita," he said. "We are working on various measures to provide liquidity to the economy and you'll see that soon, but the IMF is not an option."

Oddsson also voiced a blunt opposition to an IMF program in his famous TV interview on October 7. He claimed the IMF would demand that the government give up sovereignty, and claimed that the fund was a recourse for only "bankrupt nations"—which in his view Iceland was not. On the fifteenth, when CBI decided to lower the policy rate from 15.5 percent to 12 percent—in direct contradiction of the IMF plan then being prepared—some suspected the governor was attempting sabotage. In an October 23 interview with the *Financial Times*, Oddsson offered only "lukewarm support" for the IMF's rescue package, and hoped it would not end in "humiliation."

Meanwhile, it is possible to discern sound logic behind Iceland's pursuit of a loan from Russia. All other nations had rejected its pleas for help. Russia, having benefited greatly from high oil prices in the past year, had amassed nearly $600 billion in foreign reserves by mid-2008; a $5 billion loan to Iceland was small potatoes. What was more, here was a tiny island nation, a NATO founder of strategic importance, seemingly forsaken. The Kremlin likely felt the temptation to make a splash in the international press by offering a desperate country a loan.

By October, however, Russia's fortunes had reversed when oil prices dropped precipitously. Its own banking crisis had set in, and foreign reserves were shrinking. Faced with these sobering conditions, Moscow's interest in the venture seemed to fizzle as well; the loan has yet to materialize.

For Iceland, this gambit produced mixed results. Turning to Russia was really a means of demanding attention from the United States, the former cold war ally. This trick had been played successfully in the past, most notably during the Cod War of the 1970s, when NATO forced the British to back away from Iceland. A flirtation with Moscow also piqued the attention of Norway, which, after U.S. forces withdrew from their Icelandic base, was effectively in charge of the North Atlantic. Sure enough, a week after the Russian loan was announced delegations from Norway and the United States appeared. It was the beginning of a new alliance with Norway, the only ally Iceland could claim during the coming winter storms.

But the nation paid a price when its international image was further compromised by its dalliance. The old canards that had painted Iceland as some kind of laundry for Russian mafia money resurfaced. Much worse, however, was the delay that resulted from the chase of a red herring. The government, particularly the Independence Party, seemed to have wasted precious time waiting for Russian money instead of seeking out IMF assistance.

The Social Democratic leader, Ingibjörg Sólrún Gísladóttir, returned to Iceland after a successful brain surgery in the United States but was too frail to participate in the action. There was now a growing division within the government that would result in a split between the two dominant parties less than five months later. Much of the debate concerned national options and direction, but Oddsson's performance as a crisis manager was becoming a central issue as well. Now surfacing was the age-old dispute between isolationist and internationalist elements in Icelandic society. The former wanted to use the emergency law to the fullest and not accept any responsibility for the private debts of the banks, even though it meant that country would be chastised by the international financial community or the European Union.

The CBI governor had requested entrance to a cabinet meeting on the Monday after Glitnir's nationalization plan was announced. It was a day of bank downgrades, and CBI likely realized their plan had failed spectacularly. Oddsson's tone was sermonizing. He argued that the banks were doomed and that "the wall of shields" was needed to protect domestic operations—this was the tack of later emergency laws.

But Oddsson also proposed a new emergency government, in which all parties in parliament would take part. In itself, this was not a terrible idea, but Social Democrats saw it as nothing but a power play. The Independence vicechair publicly suggested that Oddsson would do well to focus on CBI's tasks and steer clear of politics.

Another confrontation occurred after the emergency law was drafted. Haarde proposed that a committee should be formed with representatives from the ministries of finance and commerce, the prime ministry, CBI, and FSA. The committee chairman? Mr. Oddsson. Again, the essence of the idea was practical, but Social Democrats were not going to allow their old adversary a shot at control of the country. Soon they were demanding that Oddsson would be relieved from his CBI post. So were angry crowds that protested every Saturday, throughout the winter.

Haarde often sounded indecisive during the crisis but he always made one thing clear: Oddsson would not be removed as CBI governor. After the banking collapse, Oddsson claimed publicly, on numerous occasions, that he had warned his peers in government repeatedly about the pending collapse—going back as far as February 2008—to no avail. Of course he blamed the "Viking raiders" who had leveraged the country abroad for the ultimate collapse. But each of his public utterances implicitly implicated his friend Haarde; after all, if the CBI governor was shouting warnings, the prime minister ought to have listened and taken action. Oddsson's critics pointed out that if he had really known what was going to happen to the banks in early 2008, it was beyond comprehension why the CBI had continued to accept "love letters"—unsecured bonds—from the banks in collateralized lending until the very day of the default. It could also be pointed out that all three of the banks actually had relatively sound Icelandic assets from their loan portfolio that could have been tendered instead of the love letters, and that CBI saw no need to request them. As it was, when the banks went into receivership and defaulted on the bonds used in the collateralized lending, the CBI lost an amount roughly equal to 25 percent of Iceland's GDP and de facto joined the banks in "technical" bankruptcy with negative equity. The first IMF fact-finding team had arrived on Sunday, October 5, one day before the emergency laws were passed. Over the coming weeks, in coordination with CBI and government officials, IMF hammered out a joint economic plan that included a $2 billion loan from the fund and $4 billion from central banks in Scandinavia, Japan, and other nations. These Samaritans were lending under the IMF's "seal of approval"; they were not lending directly to Iceland. Finally, on the twenty-seventh, after weeks of political arm-twisting, the country sought IMF assistance with the launch of an economic stabilization plan. But by then, yet another obstacle had arisen.

⇥ THE ICESAVE DISPUTE ⇤

As all-consuming as the banking crisis was, some elements of the government tried to push forward with their business. Despite Haarde's retreat and the illness of Gísladóttir, the foreign service still was promoting Iceland's candidacy to the UN Security Council. This was an effort almost four years in the making, and diplomats were determined that it would not be sunk by the toxic publicity created by ruined banks and the "terrorist state" brand. They went on wooing other small nations and arguing their case to the last. But on October 17, Austria and Turkey handily defeated Iceland in the vote after all and subjected it to yet another global bruising.

While the Icelandic diplomatic brass was treating representatives from tiny island states in the Pacific to blueberry pancakes and other Icelandic delicacies to solicit their vote for the UN security council, the British foreign service was quietly and efficiently gathering support among the other nations of the EU for a resolution to the Icesave imbroglio. Despite the utter collapse of their international standing, Icelandic officials remained evasive and ultimately uncommitted to a state guarantee for Icesave's British customers. The British also wanted more than the minimum guarantee. They wanted the same treatment that Icelandic depositors had received, a full refund for the institutional depositors to the accounts. The delay was so prolonged that the British government at last decided to pay out in full to its compromised citizens. Still determined to make Iceland pull its weight, they sent a delegation to the island to negotiate a settlement, but this effort too proved unsuccessful.

Part of the problem was that Icesave had created a hot-button political issue at home. The public, finding out that their bankers had so deeply indebted the nation abroad, was whipped into fury. After all, the number of British account holders was roughly equal to the total number of Icelanders—300,000—so in a way, all Icelanders would be saddled with their very own Icesave account to pay back; a significant sum indeed. The British claim amounted to between 60 and 80 percent of the GDP—this just seemed to be an impossible burden when the economy in general was still a wreck.

Faced down by angry constituents, the government insisted that Landsbanki assets ultimately would cover the Icesave claims and that their best position in the matter was a hands-off one. They continued to claim there was no legal basis for them to issue a full guarantee, since the Deposit Insurance Fund was the liable party. In fact, the Icelanders were smarting under the Terrorism Act, and they were determined to make any issue into a forum on which they could protest what to them was an injustice. They argued their cause at NATO meetings, and even refused to allow British fight squadrons to enter the country as part of NATO-led surveillance missions.

The British saw their own methods as an indemnity, not injustice, and they believed the stubborn, small nation needed more tough medicine, not less.

When Iceland finally filed its application to the IMF, it was blocked by the English, in collaboration with Holland, another Icesave nation. The British were also able to enlist another powerful ally, Germany, in which Kaupthing had been offering Edge accounts under an Icelandic deposit guarantee. The total owed to Edge customers in Germany was EUR 400 million, and it was never in danger of being lost; all of Iceland's German debts were to be paid in full. But for some reason, the Germans were not swayed by the numbers and gave their support to Britain as well.

This was just one front of a growing financial blockade. With foreign reserves dwindling, foreign exchange rationing, and a growing shortage of imports, the island was beginning to suffocate. The British meanwhile had managed to bring into their siege camp all other EU nations, including the Scandinavians.

The coalition had been formed as a matter of principle, and as a means to keep the Common European Market and cross-border competition in financial services intact. Banks were extending their reach throughout Europe, but with their home country's deposit guarantee as the ultimate insurance. If one nation was unable to provide this insurance abroad, there could be more disasters in store, even though a home-nation guarantee was not required in the strict, legal sense. After a year of crisis, the world was no longer willing to risk another system collapse or continental bank run because of one outlier's intransigence.

Iceland, stubborn as always, held out for a month against the inevitable. From their perspective, *they* were on the receiving end of mistreatment. Most ordinary Icelandic citizens felt as if they had been expelled from Europe.

In the end, however, there was little to do but accept the conditions dictated by their tiny size and isolation. It does not really matter what you think, after all, if the whole world is thinking otherwise.

Under threats of expulsion from the European Economic Area, the foundation of their prosperity, the Icelandic government accepted liability for the Icesave accounts on November 17. The British had conceded one demand, and the Icelanders would pay back only the minimum deposit guarantee. The IMF's plan became effective on November 20.

⇥ Always Look on the Bright Side of Life ⇤

Iceland now enjoys the dubious distinction of being the only Western nation to have "solved" its banking problem. About 85 percent of the financial system collapsed when the three banks were taken into receivership. Six months later, two-thirds of the remainder fell, and the FSA took control of a couple of savings and loan funds and the investment bank Straumur-Burdaras. The savings and loan funds were essentially out of equity (and actually more than that), but Straumur could not meet foreign refinancing by set due dates. This means that about 95 percent of the Icelandic banking system is now under state control while other Western nations are still trying to save theirs.

The three banks now operate under the old bank–new bank division outlined in the emergency law. The old banks were not brought into default but have effectively become asset management companies. The aim is to recover as much value as possible from the foreign assets of the old banks to compensate bondholders. This will take years.

The new banks are now rebuilding themselves as domestic commercial banks. The domestic assets that were transferred to them at the time of the collapse have yet to be appraised, which means that each bank has operated without a defined balance sheet over the winter of 2008–2009.

The events of 2008 have not been very kind to the loan portfolio of the banks, as would be expected from a situation that includes 100 percent currency deprecation, collapse of property prices, 95 percent wipeout of the stock market, 10 percent unemployment, terrorist sanctions, a credit freeze, double-digit inflation and so on. The majority of all businesses in Iceland are technically in default, and a enormous write-off is expected from the corporate loan books of the old banks.

There is some good news. The old bank–new bank construction is in many ways similar in practice to the bad/good division implemented in many Western countries. The government will buy the Icelandic assets from the old banks at fair value—after a realistic write-off—and the new banks might have the chance to start with a clean slate, with the loan losses left in the old banks. The asset transfer is a very delicate, complicated job; if the price is too low, the bondholders will complain of being unfairly treated, if too high, the banks will be bankrupted directly. For many of these assets no price can possibly be estimated, given the uncertainty that surrounds the Icelandic economy at this time. This is banking in a gray area that has not really been chartered before, and no one knows the final outcome. At present, it seems Iceland will have a new banking system defined by its own domestic savings pool, about equal to one to two times the GDP.

The large investment companies died one by one over the winter. Their assets were restructured and either taken into custody of the banks or just sold off. When Baugur went into default in early March 2009, Jóhannesson claimed that Oddsson had taken his "final revenge." He has been stripped of nearly all of his companies. Jóhannesson wrote an article for a leading daily titled "Did I Bankrupt Iceland?" in which he rejected the role of a major culprit in the national disaster. He has left the country, stating that Iceland needs a break from him and vice versa; like Arnold Schwarzenegger, he promises, "I'll be back."

Some investment companies remain afloat—barely—as they try desperately to close a restructuring deal with their creditors, turning debt into equity; extend the maturity of payments; and so on. For most of them, dealing with foreign creditors is easier than dealing with the new state-owned banks. Postcollapse Iceland has little patience for the "Viking raiders" who leveraged the country abroad and fast-tracked it for ruin. The former owners of Kaupthing are still claiming that their short position against the krona, taken through forward contracts with the old banks, should be balanced against its outstanding debt to them.

More worrisome is the fate of the "real" multinationals, formerly successful production companies that had been built up before the financial bubble. They are now virtually without banking service and are stigmatized by epithets like, among others, "the Nigeria of the North." The new banks have limited foreign currency, nor are they big enough to service companies on an international scale. There is real fear that these multinationals will have no access to foreign financing and will be taken over by foreign creditors in the coming months. If this comes to pass, Iceland truly will have lost everything it was working for during the internationalization of the corporate sector.

Around 60 to 70 percent of the employees of the old banks were transferred along with the domestic assets and are now working in the new banks. Most of Einarsson's top brass either were fired from the bank or left voluntarily. The bank-funded employee stock ownership program has backfired horribly since the collapse and left many personally bankrupt. It is still being debated, as debts are settled, if employees should be held personally responsible.

The IMF solution to Iceland's balance of payment problem was to impose capital controls and effectively fence the carry traders still stuck in the country. At the same time, policy rates were pushed up to 18 percent and kept level until March, when a program of cautious rate cuts began. The wisdom of implementing strict capital controls while keeping interest rates higher than any others in Europe, in the country hardest hit by the credit crisis, is questionable to say the least. The interest rate payments on the carry trade positions are invested in government securities, and are roughly equal to the revenue from the cod fishing around Iceland. The high interest rates also threaten to deepen the already steep output contraction, which forecasters predict will reach 10 to 15 percent in 2009.

With the ISK so low, Icelandic wages are now approximately 50 to 60 percent of the general wage level in Scandinavia. Private consumption has plummeted. Unemployment is now around 10 percent and much of the population is at least considering moving abroad. But with unemployment also rising rapidly in neighboring countries, opportunities away from home are hardly bountiful.

A lower ISK had provided such stimulus to exports that the country developed a trade surplus of around 5 to 10 percent of the GDP.

With the price of the primary exports—fish and aluminum—plummeting due to recession abroad, this advantage is disintegrating as well. Hope for foreign dollars is now tied to the tourists, mainly Scandinavians, who have been flocking to the island to take advantage of bargains, and perhaps, to witness the aftermath of disaster.

Once the Icesave dispute was resolved and the common enemy beyond the shores retreated, in November 2008, bankers and politicians have had no buffer from the wrath and incredulity of the population. "How the hell did you bungle this so badly?" is a question that defines their professional existence. The bankers, former darlings of the nation, are now described in the media as greedy, reckless, and even criminal. A truth commission has been appointed to re-create the events of the collapse, and a special prosecutor will investigate any crimes possibly committed in the financial market.

There is no doubt that many of the actions of the banks in the last 12 months of their existence resided in a gray area. It has yet to be determined if they were actually breaking Icelandic law or European directives in a systematic way, reckless though they might have been. Nevertheless, that does not mean the former titans can rest easy, however; investigations of this nature are rarely judged to be worthwhile if they let an entire rogues' gallery off scot-free.

The government, as Haarde's statements convey, denied any responsibility and attempted to heap all the blame on the bankers. But they could not keep public anger at bay, either. Protests outside the ministries had begun in October and gathered steam each week, even while they remained peaceful. After a brief lull through the Christmas holidays, anger burst forth anew in what would be called the "kitchen-ware revolution." Protestors banging pots and pans surrounded and all but blockaded the parliament house and shouted again and again "Incompetent government!" They demanded a new election and called for certain officials—notably Oddsson and the chief of the FSA—to resign.

There were signs that the protest might become violent once they began to attract young toughs, anarchists, and common criminals into the mix. In one instance, the peaceful (but still vociferous) protestors were needed to form a human shield around the small band of Reykjavik riot police to protect *them* against possible mob violence. This incident was exceptional (especially for Iceland, which had rarely known protest of any kind in modern history); protests in the main were orderly, without vandalism or serious injuries.

On January 24, 2009, Haarde announced his resignation after revealing that he was suffering from throat cancer. Shortly afterward, the Social Democrats defected from the government at large and formed a new minority body with the Left-Green Party. The new combine's leader, Jóhanna Sigurdardóttir (born 1942), is a seasoned Social Democrat who won distinction as the world's first openly gay minister on February 1. Sigurdardóttir was originally a labor union leader, but has 30 years of experience as an MP. An outspoken advocate of social reform and longtime critic of the extravaganzas in the corporate sector, she enjoys wide approval and a reputation for honesty.

In the elections held on April 25, the center-left parties obtained a majority in parliament for the first time in Iceland's history. Independents went down in a crushing defeat. The new government had declared that the Scandinavian-model economy, rather than freewheeling Anglo-Saxon capitalism, is the new way forward.

David Oddsson was not about to cave to the demands for his head, even while CBI was besieged by protestors. Once his party was driven from power in February, however, the new prime minister sent him a letter that called for his resignation. He did not budge, however, until a special law was passed in parliament, on February 26, that reduced the number of CBI governors from three to one, effectively terminating his position. A Norwegian specialist was brought in as a stopgap while the search continues for a permanent appointment to the governor's chair.

Beneath the hurly-burly of politics, Icelandic society has undergone its own quiet transformation. Historically, the nation adhered to egalitarianism, and there was virtually no ostentatious wealth. The banking boom changed this, and quickly, but in its aftermath values

are returning to their former patterns. While the wealthiest Icelanders have lost almost everything, many are quite relieved to find
equality restored.

There is abundant hope that a new Iceland will be built as well.
National awareness has increased, as evidenced by certain increases:
the consumption of Icelandic food is up, the birthrate is up, the sale
of books has skyrocketed, theater tickets are selling in record numbers, and so on. By losing so much and sharing in suffering with their
neighbors, people are now experiencing a new freedom granted by
the end of materialism. Education and health care remain free. The
nation is self-sufficient, in terms of both food and energy, which adds
greatly to the sense of security.

Icelandic pride has found a new medium; its people refuse to see
themselves as victims. For 20 years a nation of wannabes, they have
already begun to make new plans. In a matter of months, Iceland has
cleared away the wreckage of the multinationals and reinstated a
state-owned banking system and capital controls.

There are now two distinct camps in Icelandic politics. One sees
entrance into the Europe Union as the only hope for recapturing some
of the ephemeral international glory. The other is quite happy to return
to the old Iceland, contained in a natural, resource-based economy. To
keep order at home or push aggressively outward: it is a very familiar
choice to Icelanders, and perhaps a natural outgrowth of life on a
remote island, where the sea promises both solitude and adventure.

REYKJAVIK ON THE THAMES

On March 12, 2008, just days before the Bear Stearns rescue, the fixed income research department of Merrill Lynch, London, published a report titled "Eschatological. Time to Go Long."

"We don't expect a single default because of one simple fact: banks don't default. . . . Northern Rock, IKB, Landesbank Sachsen, Banca Italease—all point to this one fact that is supported by decades of empirical evidence. Yes, banks do fail—they fail more than corporations do, hardly surprising given their high level of gearing and the perverse incentive structure under which they operate (by which we mean banks or rather their managements have relatively little to lose by taking lots of risk and quite a lot to gain)."

Banks in the Western world have operated for decades under the assumption that both bondholders and depositors have a government guarantee against their loss. By 2008, it had been 35 years since last major bank default in Europe—*all* failed banks were saved in those years. This assumption of state support unquestionably helped to fuel the Western banking bubble, and it also helped the Icelandic banks to shine in the view of the ratings agencies.

So far, the governments have done their best to confirm the assumption by pledging their funds to the support of tottering banking sectors, even while the enormous balance sheets present a dire liability for taxpayers. The approach may work after all, but one thing is already certain: these measures can easily translate into a sovereign debt crisis.

The notable exceptions are the Lehman Brothers $120 billion default and the Iceland collapse, in which the banks collectively represented a $55 billion loss. The forsaking of Lehman is almost universally regarded as a grave mistake, but what about Iceland?

There is no denying that its bankers recklessly courted systematic risk, while the government was clueless as it faced the resulting crisis. But it is also clear that Iceland would *not* have failed so spectacularly if it had received outside help. Kaupthing might have had a fighting chance had it been taken into default by British authorities, as a counteraction to the Icesave debacle.

Be that as it may, Iceland has a new addition to its economic vocabulary—the word *kreppa*—which describes the sharp output contraction and is for all intents synonymous with "depression." The cost to the nation will soon be tallied, but the influence of this private disaster on the rest of the Western financial system remains open to speculation.

The fact that a developed economy could utterly collapse is a frightening sign of new times. Some temper the implications of the disaster by suggesting that Iceland was an aberration: its banking system grew to *10 times* the GDP, it is noted, while others suggest that exceptional stupidity or criminality were root causes.

We can say for certain *how* the collapse happened. Iceland's banks were taken down by a systemwide bank run that was touched off when the financial system lost the confidence of foreign creditors and analysts. Perhaps economic theory would declare this outcome inevitable, given that the nation had its own currency, almost no foreign reserves, and a central bank that could not serve as a credible lender of last resort. The state's taxing power was also insufficient to provide bank support by recapitalizing the banks or guaranteeing their deposits abroad.

The collapse demonstrated key failings of the Common European Market, and corrective efforts are already under way, such as a reform of deposit insurance in the European Economic Area.

More controversial, and perhaps influential, is the UK invocation of terrorist legislation against a commercial bank. The British financial sector continues to mull the implications of this drastic measure, and some fear the precedent might compromise London's status as the world's financial capital. Since authorities did not hesitate to employ the extraordinary powers granted for combating terrorism, they may well do it again if another drastic intervention in financial markets seems justified. Will this compromise their relations with foreign banks and governments?

After all, Iceland is not the anomaly that many would like it to be. Its plight differs more in terms of scale rather than qualitatively. Actually, there are many countries that share the following characteristics: they are (a) small countries with (b) large, internationally exposed banking sectors, (c) a currency that is not a global reserve currency, and (d) a limited fiscal capacity.

The list might even include Britain herself. William Buiter, professor at LSE, published an article in the *Financial Times* on November 13, 2008, that asked "Is London Really Reykjavik on the Thames"? Apply the characteristics just mentioned above: the UK banking sector is 4.5 times the size of the GDP, the pound is not a reserve currency, and foreign reserves stand at a relatively miniscule $43 billion. Could Britain be exposed to the twin menace of a currency and banking crisis, and the subsequent loss of confidence? What about Switzerland, another nation with its own currency, limited taxing power and oversized banking system?

Another casualty (although not a mortal one) of the recent crisis, Ireland, would have been helpless without its EU membership and the euro. Its banks also faced a run on deposits in the wake of Lehman's fall, and the government responded with a blanket guarantee, inside and beyond national borders, amounting to about double of Ireland's GDP. This was a gamble, since the Irish state would have been drowned by claims had the guarantee ever been called in. But with the backing of the union, the move to assure depositors was more credible, and ultimately successful. Nevertheless, there is the whiff of gallows' humor about the well-circulated joke that claims the difference between Iceland and Ireland was one letter and six months.

In Eastern Europe, too, there is a real danger that any number of nations might emulate Iceland's fate. This region's banking systems are dominated by foreign banks of the West, which will call for a bailout from home or from the Eurozone. But should any such bailout fail, countries, such as Austria, whose banks are heavily exposed to Eastern Europe, would face serious problems. Even Russia, bolstered by $600 billion in foreign reserves in mid-2008, has suffered a meltdown and currency outflows.

Potential trouble, in other words, still plagues much of Europe. The residual costs of the big three central banks' decision to let Iceland fail may be extensive, and there is continued risk of a domino effect. "Going Iceland" is now synonymous with systemic collapse, and hardly a week passed in the winter of 2008–2009 without some European government being forced to deny they were going that fine way themselves. Just as Lehman's fall seems to have marked the end of the broker-dealer model of large, independent investment banks with no retail financing, Iceland's demise has undermined the credibility of the smaller European financial systems, at least in regions outside the dollar and euro areas.

It is still too early to gauge the depth and direction of the trouble that was caused when the system clipped off its smallest tendril. However, it seems safe to predict that all financial centers outside the big currency areas will face numerous challenges in the foreseeable future.

And there are other hazards that will arise if the WaMu-ization of Iceland actually works. Instead of bailing out its bondholders and sloughing the responsibility for the balance sheets onto taxpayers, by supplying equity to compensate for loan losses or accepting potentially worthless assets as collateral for funding, the Icelandic government turned the tables and socked it to the bondholders. It was a desperate solution, and anything but premeditated. Nevertheless, should it work it will create incentive for other countries ravaged by the asset bubble to hang their own bondholders out to dry.

As it stands, the rescue packages on both sides of the Atlantic carry a real risk of bankrupting the governments that assembled them, should the financial system continue to disintegrate. This would be the case if the amount of deleveraging needed to resuscitate finance is simply too large in comparison with the fiscal capacity of the governments.

It may well be that Iceland was the canary in the coal mine, in life as well as death.

INDEX